A Modern Twist
Create Quilts with a Colorful Spin

Natalie Barnes

WITH ANGELA WALTERS

Martingale
Create with Confidence

DEDICATION

This book is for "the girls." They stuck together through thick and thin. Grandma Stephanie taught me how to see only the beauty in every simple thing. Aunt Laura Marie showed me how to say "yes" to life. And my mother, Norma Rose, demonstrated the benefits of unwavering kindness. Beauty, enthusiasm, and kindness fill the days of my life; thank you for these lessons. They serve me well.

Author's grandmother Stephanie

A Modern Twist: Create Quilts with a Colorful Spin
© 2015 by Natalie Barnes with Angela Walters

Martingale®
19021 120th Ave. NE, Ste. 102
Bothell, WA 98011-9511 USA
ShopMartingale.com

Printed in China

20 19 18 17 16 15   8 7 6 5 4 3 2 1

Library of Congress Cataloging-in-Publication Data available upon request.

ISBN: 978-1-60468-499-5

MISSION STATEMENT

Dedicated to providing quality products and service to inspire creativity.

CREDITS

PUBLISHER AND CHIEF VISIONARY OFFICER
Jennifer Erbe Keltner

EDITORIAL DIRECTOR
Karen Costello Soltys

DESIGN DIRECTOR
Paula Schlosser

ACQUISITIONS EDITOR
Karen M. Burns

PHOTOGRAPHER
Brent Kane

TECHNICAL EDITOR
Ellen Pahl

PRODUCTION MANAGER
Regina Girard

COPY EDITOR
Marcy Heffernan

ILLUSTRATOR
Missy Shepler

SPECIAL THANKS
Martingale thanks Elke and Don Spivey for generously alllowing the photography of this book to take place in their home.

A Million Thanks

If you take away any one thing from this book, I hope it's that we are the sum of our parts. We truly stand shoulder to shoulder, and we are better for it. When you start to build your quilting toolbox, be sure you start with your quilting friends. Years ago I received a call from Martingale author Rose Hughes, just phoning to check in on me. Her timing, of course, was perfect. I had just returned from spreading my mother's ashes atop the Santa Rosa Mountains. "What are you sewing?" she asked. "Nine patches," I answered. "Why?" and I replied, through my tears, "Because I can." To this day, we still call to check on each other, 20 years later.

I am ever so thankful to the whole team at Martingale. They are an encouraging, positive bunch. From the initial introduction, to the final marketing of the books they publish, many hands touch a book. Take a look at all of the names on the opposite page. This is the team that brings you great quilting and knitting books. Thank you, Martingale, for believing in this title.

I am truly blessed to have a team of really good friends who believe in me. Thank you, Lisa and Katey, for sitting around the dining-room table and sewing with me. Thank you, Rose Hughes and Amy Ellis, for helping me sort out the process-driven aspects of writing a quilting book. And thank you to author Jill Marie Landis for reminding me to be true to my own voice. Thanks to my Hunter|Hughes business partner and good friend John, for his work with a red pen and for answering my question, "I know you're not a quilter, but if you looked at all of this, do you think that you could make this project?"

A great-big "million thanks" to Jane StPierre for being my stunt quilter, my human "quilt math" calculator, and my all-around good-counsel friend. This book would not have been possible without Jane. You'll see her name associated with many of the quilts, and her work is meticulous.

Another big thank-you goes to Angela Walters, not only for her contribution to this book, but for always coming to the table with solutions. Thank you for saying, "Yes!" before I even finish the sentence. This is the sense of community that will allow quilting to continue to grow and flourish. Finally, a big thank-you to all of you, the readers, the quilters, the sewists, the parents, the grandfolks! Whether we meet at a quilt show, or in a class, or we chat online, I am always happy to hear from you! What fun would all of this be if we couldn't share it?

Contents

Color + Contrast + Composition in Design

For much of my adult life, I worked in the field of commercial architecture and corporate interior design. I worked in the heart of the City of Angels, downtown Los Angeles, and on projects in most of the surrounding cities as well. I worked long hours for demanding clients and had precious little time for anything else. Quilting was my artistic outlet. I joined a quilt guild, took classes, and worked on a few committees. I became a part of a friendship group. The guild was a place to gather, tell stories, and find support for the work we wanted to accomplish.

Today, I am proud to say I'm a designer of quilt patterns and the owner of my business, beyond the reef. My background in architecture and design, however, still plays an important role in the design of my quilts. The math is a little different, and the construction materials softer, but I still look for the order in the random and the modern in the design.

I believe it is the resurgence of interest in mid-century modern art and architecture that has fueled modern quilting, along with the desire to create anew. We have new heroes; it is a new time in our history. It's time to create a history of quilts that reflects our appreciation of the melding of old and new.

In the early 1980s, an artist in Ohio named Nancy Crow was taking the quilting world by storm with her new quilts. She worked primarily in solids, used a big quilting stitch, and her piecing was intuitive. By the 1990s, a woman named Gwen Marston was teaching us how to work in the "liberated quiltmaking" style. She introduced us to the utilitarian quilts of the scrap-basket era and taught us how to incorporate that process into our own quilt tops. In the mid-1990s, the world of home quilting was introduced to another studio artist, Denyse

Schmidt. She was a former graphic designer turned quilter, who had studied at the Rhode Island School of Design. All of these quilters published books that gave us instructions for making their style of quilts. In 2005, we were exposed to the decades of work by Yoshiko Jinzenji from Japan and a variety of techniques that she used. Today the list of quilters who inspire us is continually growing.

If we want to make new quilts, we need new tools in our toolbox. We need a better understanding about color and color theory. We have to learn how to create contrast with the scale of the new fabrics that are being designed, or we need to let go of the thought that we always need to create contrast. Finally, we need to "go back to school" and learn a little more about composition. Why do we create in the scale we do? Why did we put that line there? What is that circle doing over there? While the answers to *all* of these questions won't be found in this book, hopefully I'll pique your interest in the subject of modern design, color, contrast, and composition.

Machine quilting has also become a large part of the design of our quilts. Instead of selecting batting for needling by hand, we look at the loft to see how our machine-quilted patterns will shadow. We look at thread colors and wonder how they'll impact the colors in the fabrics. And we choose quilted patterns and designs that will enhance our pieced top. Long-arm machine quilting is more readily available, and more people are trying free-motion quilting on their home machines. We have embraced this technology into our modern quilting vernacular.

In this book, I've invited Angela Walters, a revolutionary professional machine quilter, to share her thoughts on how the quilting interacts with the three elements of design.

As for *A Modern Twist*? Along the way, I discovered that if you make asymmetrical blocks, and rotate them as you set them, your quilts will look much more complicated than they really are. I've used this approach in the quilts that are made up of blocks. In other quilts, the overall design is random, but with an underlying order. It's my hope that you will read through this book, make at least some of the projects, and give the concept of modern twist a try while working on color, contrast, and composition.

Happiest days,

Natalie
be. do. create.

Color + Contrast + Composition in Quilting

BY ANGELA WALTERS

"It's not a quilt until it's quilted." What an accurate statement. Whether we like it or not, the quilting stitches are an integral part of the quiltmaking process. The quilting can either add to or detract from your quilt top. I always like to joke that quilting is a lot like makeup. Makeup can enhance a face or be distracting. Even if you know this to be true, you may be unsure about how to choose the right quilting designs.

Throughout this book, Natalie discusses how to use color, contrast, and composition in your quilts. In this section, I've included suggestions and ideas on how to use the quilting itself to complement these concepts. My hope is that by sharing my thought process for choosing quilting designs, I will make it easier for you to select the perfect quilting design for each of your own quilts.

Color

Color plays a huge role in a quilter's life. One of my favorite parts of making a quilt is deciding what fabrics and colors to use. But when it comes to picking thread colors for the quilting, it's all about the quilt. Personally, I love quilting that blends in with the quilt top. This allows the quilting to enhance the quilt, without being overwhelming. Using a blending thread color also allows me to get away with dense quilting.

In "Triangle Line" on page 47, not only is the quilting fairly dense, but I also used several different designs such as wavy lines and angular squares. The matching thread lets you see the texture of the quilting without overwhelming the quilt top.

Picking the perfect thread color may seem easier said than done, but it's not too hard to choose the "right" color.

The thread color blends with the quilt in "Triangle Line."

Before I start quilting, I lay a few thread options over the quilt. I look for a thread color that blends in the best. If there are a couple of close options, I usually opt for the lighter thread color.

There are times when a quilt has too much contrast in color for just one thread color to work. Perhaps the quilt is black and white or made with contrasting solid fabrics. In those instances, I'll use more than one thread color. It may take a little longer, but the result is well worth it.

Contrast

When talking about the theory of quilting, my favorite subject is contrast. I think that some of the most striking quilts are made of highly contrasting fabrics. I also think that having contrast within the quilting is just as striking. It's amazing how contrasting quilting designs can enhance or camouflage areas of a quilt. When it comes to quilting designs, there are three main factors that determine contrast: thread color, shape, and the density of the quilting.

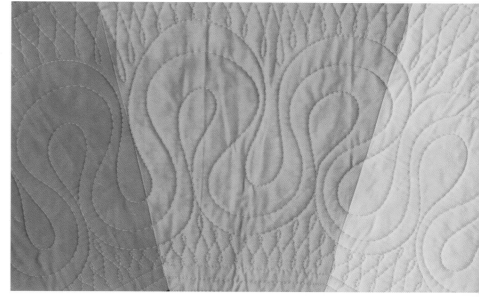

Use contrast in the density of the quilting to highlight specific areas of a quilt, as in "Color Fusion" on page 26.

The first and easiest way to provide contrast with quilting is to use a thread that's a different color than the quilt top. This allows the quilting to be seen and take center stage. Although I don't normally use thread that contrasts with the quilt top, you may want to do this if the quilting is an important element of the quilt design.

The shape of a quilting design is another area that can help provide contrast. When two different quilting designs appear next to each other on a quilt, designs that are shaped differently won't blend together as much as two designs that are similar. An example of this would be pairing curvy swirls with angular designs, or straight lines next to pebbles.

When picking the quilting designs for a quilt, I almost always think about the shape of the designs and how much contrast is needed for the quilt. For instance, using contrasting designs can help draw attention to certain areas of the quilt block that I want to highlight.

Third, and most important, changing the density between two designs is a fast and effective way to achieve contrast. You've more than likely already seen this on some quilts. The quilter who uses dense quilting around a specific motif or custom design is using the contrast in density to help the motif stand out.

When quilting "Color Fusion" (page 26 and detail on page 9), I used contrast in the density of the quilting to highlight the custom quilting design in the outer ring. Since I felt that the main motif was the most important part of the quilting, I wanted to make sure it stood out from the rest of the quilting. To fill around the motif, I quilted a figure-eight design much smaller and denser than the central motif.

Even though providing contrast within the quilting is a great way to enhance areas of your quilt, sometimes the opposite is true as well. You may want to use designs that are similar in color, shape, and density so that they are a little more muted and not so obvious. No matter what effect you are going for on your quilts, knowing how to use contrast within the quilting designs will help you achieve your goal.

The more prominent neutral area of "Resting Line" was enhanced by a larger, more complex design.

Composition

Planning the perfect quilt relies heavily on the process of composition. What layout to use? What size to make the blocks? These are questions that all quilters find themselves pondering. Once the perfect composition is decided upon, it's up to the quilting to make the composition of the quilt as effective as possible. Thankfully, that's pretty easy to do.

Like all other aspects of quilting, I find that the best way to enhance the composition of the quilt is to take my cue from the quilt itself. In larger, more open areas of a quilt, I'll use bigger, more complex designs. On the other hand, in smaller areas, I might use less complicated designs.

"Resting Line" (page 66 and details right) is the perfect example of this. The composition of this quilt is just stunning. I love the look of the skinnier colored pieces next to the large neutral strip that divides the quilt. Since the large central strip is such a prominent part of the quilt, I wanted to enhance it with a larger-scale design that was more intricate than the rest of the quilting. When it came to quilting the colored-stripe sections of the quilt, I opted for simpler motifs. The back-and-forth lines and ribbon-candy motifs are not only fast and easy, they create a nice contrast.

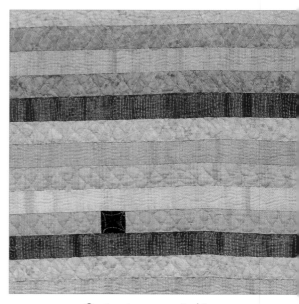

Contrast was created in "Resting Line" by using simple designs in the narrower pieced areas of the quilt.

Your turn! I hope you feel inspired and eager to use your quilting to enhance the color, composition, and contrast of your quilts. I truly hope that it's not intimidating. The art of quilting, from start to finish, is meant to be fun and stress-free. Do what you think looks good and be proud of it!

Happy quilting!

Angela

COLOR

A thimbleful of red is redder than a bucketful.
—Henri Matisse

Just as there is "quilting math," I think we should say there is "quilting color." As quilters, we work with commercially available fabrics in colors that are selected for us by our favorite pattern designers and created by our favorite fabric companies.

Seeing Color

Our eyes can see vast ranges of color, a discernible 10 million, to be clear, even though there are only about 30 names for the colors that we typically refer to when speaking about color. It is our heart, most of the time, that tells us what we like, what really appeals to us. When I was a little girl, if you asked me what my favorite color was, I would quickly say, "Purple!" As I grew older, and started painting, it became magenta, mauve, or violet, depending on whether it was Windsor and Newton or Sennelier or another brand of oil paints I was working with. Today, I'll tell you I love a Denyse Schmidt yellow. It's a clear sunshine yellow that's not too gold, and not too green. And I just love the driftwood browns that Hoffman California Fabrics uses in their collections. The palette used in Anna Maria Horner's last line had some wonderful dark-value prints that I want to use in my next scrap quilt. Lotta Jansdotter's pink has just the right touch of salmon-orange to make it completely different from any other pink I have ever seen! Now we're talking about quilting color!

We are so fortunate to have such great designers and such fabulous fabric companies working on color on our behalf. They follow color trends, scour the commercial color systems for just the right hue, value, and saturation, and then work with the fabric mills to create those pieces that we just hate to cut up! But since color plays a big role in our quilts, adding to our own knowledge base is well worth the time invested.

In visual perception a color is almost never seen as it really is—as it physically is.
—Josef Albers, *Interaction of Color*

Classic books on color are recommended time and time again. One of my very favorites is *Interaction of Color,* by Josef Albers. Yale University Press put out a 50th Anniversary Edition since the first edition was published in 1963. For most people who have studied art, this is a textbook. But don't let that scare you off. It's really a book containing a series of exercises that show us how we *see* color, rather than a textbook explaining the technical aspects of color.

The series of exercises in the book, and the color-plate examples, show what happens "between colors." Put a gold piece of fabric on turquoise adjacent to blue; put the same gold on orange adjacent to yellow. The same gold fabric, to most people, will probably look like two different colors! This is s*eeing* color.

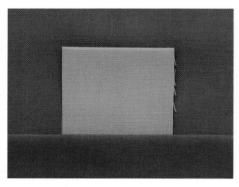 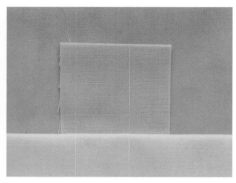

The same color can appear to be two different colors, depending on the surrounding colors..

As quilters, we add and subtract and revise and ponder and play with all of the fabrics in our stash, not just within one designer's collection of fabrics. While doing this, you'll notice that some color combinations will actually *vibrate*. You'll also see that if you use one red fabric and you put it next to turquoise, it will look like a completely different shade of red than if you placed it next to orange. These are good examples of seeing color, and this color knowledge will come in handy.

Start with the Color Wheel

The color wheel is a great place to start learning about color, and making a color wheel from fabric is one of the first projects in this book (page 26). The color wheel is composed of primary, secondary, and tertiary colors.

- **Primary colors** are the pure hues of yellow, red, and blue.

- **Secondary colors** are made from equal amounts of primary colors, and are orange, violet, and green.

- **Tertiary colors** are made from a primary color and the adjacent secondary color. They are red-orange, yellow-orange, yellow-green, blue-green, blue-violet, and red-violet.

The relationships of colors on the color wheel make up various color schemes.

- **Complementary colors** are any two colors located opposite each other on the color wheel, such as red and green.

- **Analogous colors** are two or more colors that are adjacent to each other on the color wheel, such as violet and red-violet.

- **Monochromatic colors** are made up of a single color used in various tints and shades (lights and darks).

Complementary combination

Analogous combination

Monochromatic combination

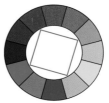

Split complementary colors   Triad colors   Tetrad colors

- **Split complementary colors** consist of a primary color and the two colors located adjacent to the complementary color.

- **Triad colors** are any three colors spaced equidistant on the color wheel.

- **Tetrad colors** are four colors that are sets of complements or sets of split complements.

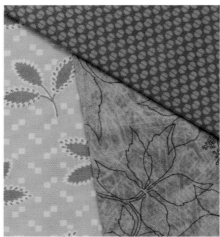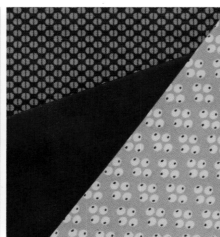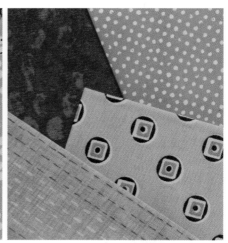

Split complementary combination: red, yellow-green, and blue-green

Triad combination: green, violet, and orange

Tetrad combination: red-violet, red-orange, yellow-green, and blue-green

Let's talk about some color basics and the terms commonly used in color discussions. These will help you in thinking about colors and fabrics for your quilts—quilting color.

- **Hue** is the technical term for color. (What hue is that? It's the color red.)

- **Saturation** is the strength or purity of a color without the addition of black or white.

- **Value** is the lightness or darkness of a color.

- **Tint** is a pure color with white added, making it a lighter value.

- **Shade** is a pure color with black added, making it a darker value.

- **Color temperature** refers to the perceived "warm" and "cool" qualities of color. Warm colors, such as red, are the colors of a welcoming sunset. Cool colors, like blue, are the colors of refreshing waters and tropical foliage.

Using Color

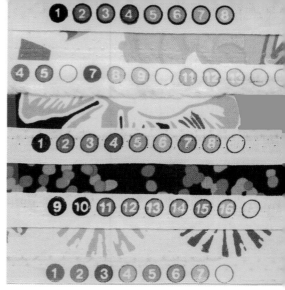

This section outlines very basic color information, and it may seem too dry or too overwhelming. After all, what you really want to do is make a beautiful quilt, bag, or other project for your home. But if you want something to coordinate with your lounge chair or contrast with your sofa, these theories will come in handy.

If you look at your quilts, you'll probably see one or more of these color combinations. If you pull out some of your favorite fabrics, you'll begin to recognize all of the hard work put into selecting just the right colors, and you'll know why the fabric designers chose them! Here's a hint: Take a look at the selvage of your printed fabrics. Fabric companies will usually include a sample of each color used in printing the fabrics. These color windows, color tabs, or dots are a great reference for matching a specific color in a multicolored print. Try using these dots to help select fabrics from other manufacturers' lines that match or coordinate with the colors in the fabric you want to work with.

Finally, there are two additional categories of color that I would add to the mix of quilting color. Maybe you've heard these terms in a class: ugly colors and magic colors.

Ugly colors are those that contrast in saturation from the colors used in a particular color scheme. For example, if you're working with all bright colors, an ugly color would be a fabric in a color that is a little less saturated than the rest of the colors in your palette. If your fabrics are all modern prints, a 1930s feedsack print would be your ugly print. If you have colors that are less saturated or are of a dark shade, the ugly color would be a saturated color.

Magic colors are unexpected colors that really go with nothing else in the selected color scheme. I think the founders of the Little Quilts shop—Mary Ellen Von Holt, Alice Berg, and Sylvia Johnson—originally coined the term in the 1980s. The magic color in my quilt "Hexagon Scramble" on page 34, which is primarily Halloween colors, is the bright pink. When you think of Halloween, you typically think of oranges, grays, and blacks, maybe even a dark purple. Pink brings to mind spring, bunnies, sundresses, and sandals.

Whether you want to add an ugly color or a magic color, work on a design wall if possible. These additional and unexpected colors are to be used sparingly, as a . . . well . . . a zinger! A surprise. A treasure. An unexpected gem.

Take your time when working on a quilt, and as Martingale author Rose Hughes would say, "Play." Pull out some fabrics and try different combinations. Put a zinger in one of your quilts. See if there's a place you can include an unexpected gem.

Use the colors in the selvages to help select coordinating fabrics.

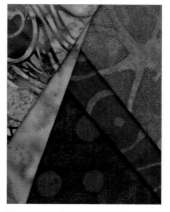

The muted tan may seem ugly, but it brings a lighter value to the grouping.

A pop of bright green works as a magic color with a group of peach prints.

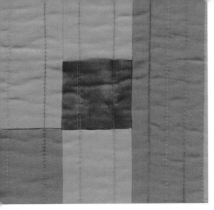

RECTANGLE CONFETTI

Seeing just one little 2½" square in just the right color can make my heart sing! I made this quilt with a splash of accent squares against a background of monochromatic solids. The writing of this book coincided with a gorgeous season of sunsets on the southern California coast where I live, inspiring the color scheme of this interpretive landscape. I literally pulled out all of the turquoise, blue, gold, and orange scraps I could find and began cutting them into squares and rectangles. Make this quilt your own with the scraps you have on hand.

Designed, made, and quilted by Natalie Barnes.
Fabrics by Hoffman California Fabrics and Robert Kaufman Fabrics.

Finished wall hanging: 18½" x 42½"
Finished block: 6" x 14"

Materials

Yardage is based on 42"-wide fabric. Fat quarters are approximately 18" x 21" and fat eighths are 9" x 21".

1 fat quarter *each* of 8 different shades or textures of blue fabrics for background
1 fat eighth *each* of 4 different contrasting-color fabrics for accent squares*
⅓ yard of print for binding
1⅓ yards of fabric for backing
24" x 48" piece of batting

You can use scraps; you'll need 31 squares, 2½" x 2½".

Cutting

From *each* of the 8 blue fabrics, cut:
3 strips, 2½" x 21"; crosscut into:
    5 rectangles, 2½" x 4½" (40 total; 3 are extra)
    1 rectangle, 2½" x 6½" (8 total)
    2 rectangles, 2½" x 8½" (16 total; 2 are extra)
    1 square, 2½" x 2½" (8 total; 4 are extra)

From *each* of the 4 accent fabrics, cut:
1 strip, 2½" x 21"; crosscut into 8 squares,
    2½" x 2½" (32 total; 1 is extra)

From the binding print, cut:
4 strips, 2¼" x 42"

Making the Blocks

Two different blocks make up this wall hanging. They've been rotated and flipped to distribute the accent squares, and to make the wall hanging appear more random than it really is. You'll make five of block A and four of block B. Select the pieces for each block before sewing. Referring to the block diagrams, arrange the pieces on a design wall until you're pleased with the layout. Return each completed block to the design wall and refer to them as you select pieces for each subsequent block. Press the seam allowances to the side or open as directed in the diagrams.

MAKING BLOCK A

1 Arrange the assorted blue pieces and the accent squares in three rows as shown on page 18. Sew three blue 2½" x 4½" rectangles together with one accent 2½" square to form the top row. Sew one blue 2½" x 8½" rectangle, one accent 2½" square, and one blue 2½" x 4½" rectangle together as shown to form the middle row. Sew

one blue 2½" x 4½" rectangle, one blue 2½" x 8½" rectangle, and one accent 2½" square together for the bottom row.

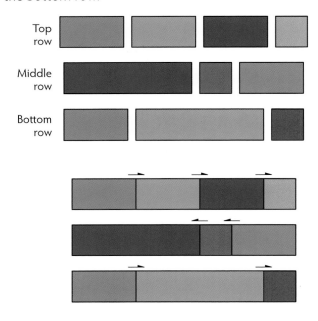

Top row

Middle row

Bottom row

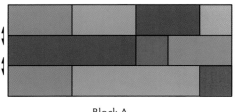

2 Sew the three rows together to make block A. Repeat to make a total of five of block A.

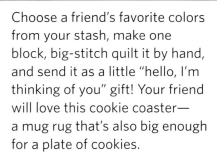

Block A.
Make 5.

MAKING BLOCK B

1 Arrange the assorted blue pieces and the accent squares in three rows as shown. Sew two accent 2½" squares, one blue 2½" x 4½" rectangle, and one blue 2½" x 6½" rectangle as shown to form the top row. Sew one blue 2½" x 4½" rectangle, two accent 2½" squares, and one blue 2½" x 6½" rectangle together as shown to form the middle row. Sew one blue 2½" x 8½" rectangle, one blue 2½"square and one blue 2½" x 4½" rectangle together to make the bottom row.

Top row

Middle row

Bottom row

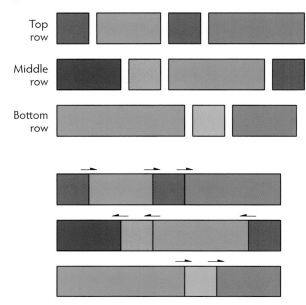

QUILTED GREETING

Choose a friend's favorite colors from your stash, make one block, big-stitch quilt it by hand, and send it as a little "hello, I'm thinking of you" gift! Your friend will love this cookie coaster—a mug rug that's also big enough for a plate of cookies.

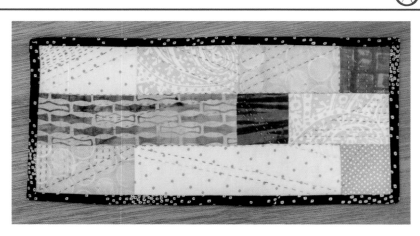

2 Sew the three rows together to make block B. Repeat to make a total of four of block B.

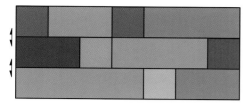

Block B.
Make 4.

Assembling and Finishing

1 Refer to the quilt assembly diagram and arrange the blocks on a design wall, or another available flat surface, in three horizontal rows of three blocks each. Sew the blocks together in rows, matching all seam intersections. Pin for accuracy, removing pins as you sew. Press seam allowances in opposite directions from row to row. Sew the rows together, pinning again for accuracy, to complete your quilt top. Press the remaining seam allowances in one direction.

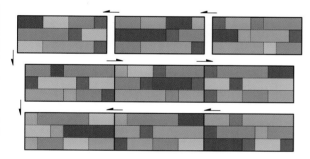

Quilt assembly

2 Referring to "Backing" on page 74, prepare the backing by cutting a piece that is 24" x 48". If you choose to send your top to be quilted by a long-arm machine quilter, check with the quilter for specific requirements for backing size. Adjust the backing yardage accordingly.

3 Refer to "Quilt" on page 74 and "Finish" on page 77 for further instructions on quilting options, basting, and binding. Be sure to add a label to your quilt.

This version of "Rectangle Confetti" is hand quilted and made completely of scraps.

STUDIO BOXES

Some people work best in an organized and structured environment. Others work in less orderly surroundings, with lots of stimuli. Which type of quilter are you? Even if you like lots of fabrics and tools and books and photographs, it's nice to have containers to group similar items together. Make a few of these boxes in different colors, and fill them with scraps or fat quarters. They also make a great gift, filled with a friend's favorite-color fabric bundles!

Designed and made by Natalie Barnes. Fabrics by Alexander Henry Fabrics, Robert Kaufman Fabrics, and Hoffman California Fabrics.

Finished box: 5½" x 8½" x 5½"

Materials

Materials are for 1 box. Yardage is based on 42"-wide fabric. Fat quarters are approximately 18" x 21".

1 fat quarter of fabric for outer box
1 fat quarter of fabric for lining
⅛ to ¼ yard *total* of assorted scraps for outer
   box sides
18" x 21" piece of fusible fleece

Cutting

From the assorted scraps, cut:*
4 strips, 2" x 10"
4 strips, 1½" x 10"
4 strips, 1" x 10"

*Feel free to vary the strip widths as desired.

Making the Box

You'll use the Quilt as You Go method to make the boxes. Refer to "Quilt as You Go" on page 25 for detailed instructions.

1 Trim the selvage from each of the fat quarters, and then trim the fat quarters and fusible fleece as needed to make sure the corners are square and that all are the same size rectangle.

2 Fuse the fleece to the wrong side of the fabric for the outer box, following the manufacturer's instructions.

3 Cut a 6" x 6" square from each corner as shown. Trim the lining fat quarter in the same manner.

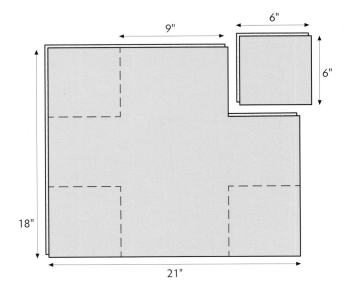

4 With the fabric for the outer box facing up, begin adding strips to the edge of one of the 9" sides using the Quilt as You Go technique. After sewing the last strip near the center, fold the raw edge under so that it's even with the 6" sides and sew next to the folded edge. Trim the ends of the strips so that they are even with the side edges. Repeat to add strips to the opposite 9" side.

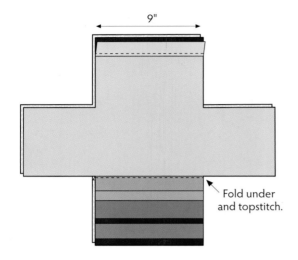

Fold under and topstitch.

5 Place the lining piece right sides together with the quilted piece. Stitch around the edges, leaving a 5" opening on one of the 9" sides. Clip inner corners and trim the outer corners.

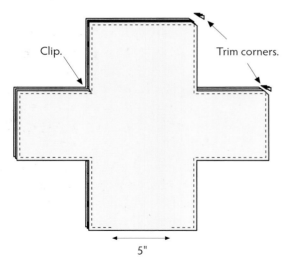

Clip.

Trim corners.

5"

6 Turn the piece right side out, and use a bamboo chopstick or other blunt tool to gently push the corners out so they're square. With a needle and thread, stitch the opening closed by hand. Press.

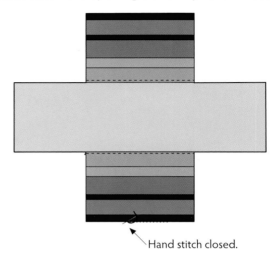

Hand stitch closed.

7 With the outside edges together, align the 6" sides and stitch them together using a ¼" seam allowance. Backstitch at the beginning and end to secure the seam. Repeat on all four sides. Your box is now ready to fill!

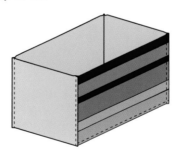

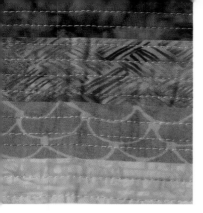

RANDOM LANDSCAPE

Nature is always an inspiration—a peaceful lake, the quiet of snow, or even a colorful sunset. Some of these moments are especially nice to remember if you've spent them with friends. Select some fabrics that remind you of a particular landscape or a special moment, and make these place mats and coasters as a reminder of that time. Wouldn't these be a wonderful thank-you gift for your friends after spending a weekend with them at their beach house? Remember, this is an exercise in interpretation, not imitation. Enjoy the process.

Designed and made by Natalie Barnes, quilted by Jane StPierre. Fabrics by Hoffman California Fabrics.

Finished place mats: 11½" x 16½"
Finished coasters: 5½" x 5½"

Materials

Materials are for 6 place mats and 6 coasters. Yardage is based on 42"-wide fabric unless otherwise noted. Fat quarters are approximately 18" x 21".

6 fat quarters of fabric in colors that represent your landscape for place-mat and coaster tops
1⅛ yards of fabric for binding
1⅓ yards of fabric for backing*
1⅝ yards of fusible fleece, such as Thermolam (45" wide)

Choose a fabric that will allow the place mats and coasters to be reversible.

Cutting

From *each* of the 6 fat quarters, cut:
3 strips, 2" x 18"
3 strips, 3" x 18"
3 strips, 1" x 6"
3 strips, 2" x 6"

From the backing fabric, cut:
6 rectangles, 12" x 17"
6 squares, 6" x 6"

From the binding fabric, cut:
16 strips, 2¼" x 42"

From the fusible fleece, cut:
6 rectangles, 12" x 17"
6 squares, 6" x 6"

Making the Place Mats

Determine the color order for your strips. For my sunset place mats and coasters, I used a warm sand color along the bottom to represent the sunset reflecting off of the wet sand. Next to that I placed three orange fabrics from light to dark for the sunset, and then a medium and a dark violet for the dark sky above. You'll be quilting as you create the place mats, so refer to "Quilt as You Go" on page 25 for helpful hints before proceeding.

1 Referring to the manufacturer's instructions, fuse the wrong side of the backing to the fusible side of the fleece. Once you have fused the two together, turn your piece over so that the fleece is right side up and the backing is right side down.

2 Select one strip of each color, for a total of three 3" x 18" strips and three 2" x 18" strips. Once you are sure of the color order and composition, keep the order the same for each of the place mats.

3 Place the first strip right side up on the fleece, along the 17" side. Place the second strip right

sides together with the first, aligning the raw edges. Using a leader or scrap of folded fabric (see page 73 for additional details), sew together through all layers with a ¼" seam allowance. Stitch off of your place mat onto a second leader; snip the threads between the leader and the layered piece and remove the layered piece from the machine. Flip the seam open and finger-press, or press with an iron.

4 Using a leader as in step 3, stitch through the fabric strips and through all layers with a vertical line parallel to the 17" side of your piece. Rotate the piece and sew a second line through the strip. Continue quilting lines through the strip until you like the look. The number of lines you quilt in the strip will depend on the width of the strip and your personal preference. Stitch in opposite directions from one line of quilting to the next to ensure your piece will remain square.

5 Repeat the process to add another strip, continuing until the whole piece is covered.

6 Trim and square up the place mat to 11½" x 16½".

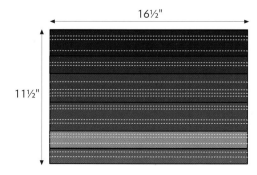

7 Repeat steps 1–6 to make a total of six place mats.

Making the Coasters

1 Follow steps 1–5 of "Making the Place Mats" on page 23 using the 6" squares of fleece and fabric. Add the 1" x 6" and 2" x 6" strips. Make six coasters.

2 Trim and square up the coasters to 5½" x 5½".

Finishing Your Place Mats and Coasters

Refer to "Finish" on page 77 for further instructions on binding your place mats and coasters. If you like, add a label to the back of one of your place mats. You now have a new set of place mats with matching coasters. If you want to set a more serene table, turn the place mats over and use the plain backing, or mix and match as you like!

QUILT AS YOU GO

With this method, you quilt the layers as you add and sew strips together. Take your time and treat each piece as you would a quilt.

1. Cut backing and batting larger than the finished piece, unless directed otherwise.
2. Baste the backing to the batting by fusing or pinning the two layers together.
3. Lengthen the stitch on your machine and insert a new quilting or top-stitch needle. Use a walking foot for best results.
4. Check thread tension by first sewing on some scraps of your fabric and batting.
5. Reduce the presser-foot pressure if your machine offers that option.
6. Place fabric strips over the batting and backing pieces. Sew with right sides together, open up, press, and add quilting stitches. Continue until batting is covered.
7. Trim your project to size as directed.

COLOR FUSION

Color is one of the tools quilters work with every day. You'll have fun making this fabric version of the color wheel. It will be a great addition to your quilting studio, thrown over a chair, or used as a table topper. Refer to it often, and let it inspire you to work in a color scheme that you've never tried before.

Designed and made by Natalie Barnes, quilted by Angela Walters. Fabrics by Windham Fabrics and Dear Stella Design.
Finished quilt: 38½" x 38½"

Materials

Yardage is based on 42"-wide fabric. Fat quarters are approximately 18" x 21".

1 fat quarter *each* of red, yellow, blue, green, orange, violet, yellow-green, blue-green, blue-violet, red-violet, red-orange, and yellow-orange solid
1 fat quarter *each* of small-scale print in red, yellow, blue, green, orange, violet, yellow-green, blue-green, blue-violet, red-violet, red-orange, and yellow-orange
⅜ yard of gray solid for binding
1⅜ yards of fabric for backing
44" x 44" piece of batting
Creative Grids 30° Triangle ruler (CGRSG1)

Cutting

From *each* of the solids, cut:
1 strip, 11½" x 21"; crosscut into:
    1 rectangle, 11" x 11½" (12 total)
    1 rectangle, 3" x 11½" (12 total)

From *each* of the small-scale prints, cut:
1 strip, 6½" x 21"; crosscut into 1 rectangle,
    6½" x 11½" (12 total)

From the binding fabric, cut:
4 strips, 2¼" x 42"

Making the Color Wedges

1 On a flat surface, arrange the 12 solid 11" x 11½" and 12 print 6½" x 11½" rectangles in color-wheel order, beginning with red. Refer to the color wheel on page 13 or the quilt photo on page 27. Place each complementary-color 3" x 11½" strip with its complement, the color that is opposite on the color wheel. For example, put the smaller green piece with the larger red piece and vice versa. Continue until you have all of the complementary fabrics paired with the solids and prints. Now you're ready to sew!

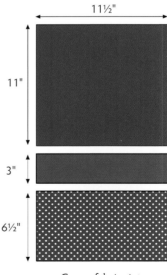

Group fabrics into
12 complementary sets.

2 Sew the red-solid 11" x 11½" rectangle, the green-solid 3" x 11½" rectangle, and the red-print 6½" x 11½" rectangle together as shown

to form one piece, 11½" x 19½". Press the seam allowances toward the strip in the middle. Continue with the remaining colors, selecting the next set of three fabrics, and sew them together.

3 Place the narrow end of the 30° triangle ruler on the print fabric, aligned with the raw edge. The seams of the 2½" strip of complementary color should align with the lines on the ruler. Using your rotary cutter, cut on each side of the ruler to make one large 30° wedge, 19½" long. Repeat for each pieced unit from step 2 to cut 12 wedges.

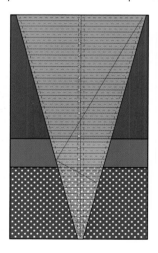

Assembling and Finishing

1 Place the wedges in color-wheel order again with red at the top. Pin the red and red-orange adjacent color-wheel wedges together, matching the 2½"-strip seams, and stitch them together.

Press the seam allowances open. Sew the wedges together in sets of three to form four "blocks," red to orange, yellows, green to blue, and violets.

2 Sew two of the blocks together in color order. Join the remaining two in the same manner, pressing the seam allowances open. Finally, sew these two pieces together, taking care to sew slowly through the bulk in the center of your piece. Press.

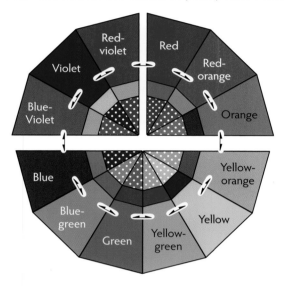

3 Prepare the backing, referring to "Backing" on page 74. If you choose to send your top to be quilted by a long-arm machine quilter, check with the quilter for specific requirements of size of backing. Adjust your backing yardage accordingly.

4 Refer to "Quilt" on page 74 and "Finish" on page 77 for further instructions on quilting options, basting, and binding. Be sure to add a label to your quilt.

CHALLENGE YOURSELF!

Keep the larger color wheel in your studio, and make a smaller one to travel with you when you are shopping for fabrics or taking a class. Challenge yourself and make an additional version of the color wheel using the printed fabrics in your stash.

CONTRAST

*I don't paint things. I only paint the
difference between things.*

—Henri Matisse

Contrast in value

Contrast in scale

Contrast in texture

Contrast in color

You've heard the sayings "a study in contrast" and "opposites attract." Whether it's the chiaroscuro in art utilizing the strong contrasts between light and dark, the variation in scale of objects, or just a rustic family heirloom sitting on a slick modern table, contrast is what sets things apart from one another. Contrast is what draws your attention to the features you want to be most noticed.

Some of the best commercial office spaces I worked on, and the spaces that I liked the best, were a grand study in contrast. Executives were sitting side by side with their engineers and assistants. Directors moved into historic buildings on movie lots and filled the spaces with Le Corbusier furniture handcrafted of stainless steel and hand-stitched black leather. Down-to-earth clothing manufacturers whose staff skateboarded to work wanted high-tech lighting and slick painted walls where before there were none. High-tech industry offices were peppered with baroque-framed oil paintings or a Chinese lacquered cabinet instead of a credenza.

I still believe it is the high-tech lamp on a chipped-paint farmhouse table that will allow you to see both items clearly. And this is a philosophy I have taken with me, out of the boardroom and into my quilting-studio life.

Create contrast in your projects, and you will see the elements of your design more clearly. What you will hear most often when quilters talk about contrast in quilting is about separation of value. Select light, medium, and dark fabrics for your projects to create contrast. Use high and low contrast, or as some people like to call it, high- and low-volume fabrics. Some of our favorite fabric and quilt designers only work in one volume—bright—and their projects are no less pleasing to us. Other days, we might see a project with very little contrast and colors in very light values, and we will think, "Oh, how restful that quilt is!" If we are taught only to use dark, medium, and light fabrics and colors in our quilts, why is it that we are so often attracted to these other projects? How do these other designers create contrast in their designs so that you are able to clearly see the various components of their quilts?

My theory about the success of these designers' work is threefold. I believe that they work well with color and understand how to manipulate it to their advantage. They know why they have used a specific color. I also believe that they have mastered the use of contrast—not just the contrast of value, but of scale and pattern also. Different sizes and shapes of pieces and varying print patterns within a quilt will create contrast just as contrasting values do. Finally, I believe that they consciously choose the composition of their projects. They purposely place an object, shape, or color in a specific location. I don't believe their seemingly random choices are random at all.

One of the last projects I worked on before retiring from designing commercial interiors was a movie producer's office. It's nothing I wouldn't say to his face—he drove everyone a little crazy in our first few project meetings. But then I realized how fortunate I was to work with someone with such attention to detail and with such an acute visual awareness.

We would review things over and over again. We would go out to the job site and look at the progress that was being made with wood, steel, and concrete. Then we would come back to the boardroom and go over it all again. And again. And the next day, after he had slept on it, we would meet and go over it yet again.

We met with the producer's feng shui consultant. We moved walls, cleared walkways, and made sure the right colors were used in the right locations.

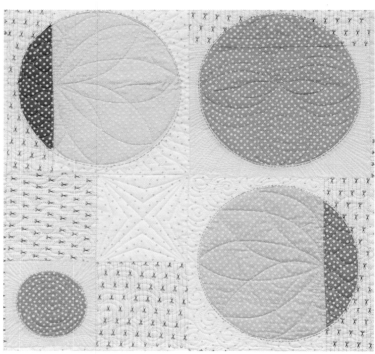

"Circle Shuffle" illustrates contrast of colors, shapes, values, and print scale. The quilting designs add contrasting textures.

When it was all done, when he moved his team into the new space, everything about it was correct. But it wasn't just correct: it was perfect. The paint colors were perfect because we looked at 15 different shades of lime green and 20 different shades of orange and brown and yellow. The colors were used in proportion to the overall envelope of the office space. The wood was in contrast to the high-tech lighting, the concrete was just the right background for large-scale lacquered mirrors leaning against bright-red walls, and the orchid plants were replaced weekly.

When you work on a quilt that's a present, you will be giving someone a gift that will last more than a lifetime. Be intentional about your choices. Even if it's intuitive, make your decisions count.

SQUARE RECTANGLE

Sometimes it's the process that creates the random. In this project, squares are used to create rectangular elements and rectangular blocks. This quilt includes one lone random block. That block is made of the same components as the others, but there's a little something different about it. This is not a humility block; besides, a mistake in an antique block probably wasn't really intentional, as some people believe. This one block is purposeful, meant to create the question in your mind, "Where is the block?"

Designed, made, and quilted by Natalie Barnes. Fabrics by Hoffman California Fabrics.

Finished quilt: 53" x 53"
Finished block: 7½" x 10½"

Materials

Yardage is based on 42"-wide fabric.

⅝ yard of gold print for accent in blocks

32 squares, 10" x 10", of assorted medium to dark prints for blocks*

8 squares, 10" x 10", of assorted orange to yellow-orange prints for blocks*

½ yard of fabric for binding

3½ yards of fabric for backing

61" x 61" piece of batting

A package of precut 10" squares may work, or you can cut squares from your stash.

CONTRAST

Contrast is the key to this design. You'll need 32 squares of similar colors and values. In addition to these, you'll need two accent colors that contrast with each other. The eight orange squares are one accent and the gold print is the second.

Cutting

From *each* of the 32 squares, cut:
5 strips, 2" x 10" (160 total; 20 are extra)

From *each* of the 8 squares, cut:
5 strips, 2" x 10" (40 total; 5 are extra)

From the gold print, cut:
2 strips, 8" x 42"; crosscut into 35 strips, 2" x 8"

From the binding fabric, cut:
6 strips, 2¼" x 42"

Making the Blocks

1 Randomly select four assorted 2" x 10" strips and one orange or yellow-orange 2" x 10" strip. Arrange the strips as shown. Sew the strips together to make a block that measures 8" x 10". Press the seam allowances in one direction. Repeat to make 35 blocks, keeping the accent strip in the same position for each block.

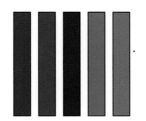 

Make 35.

2 Place one of the 8" x 10" blocks on your cutting surface with the orange accent fabric toward the top of the block as shown. Cut the block into an 8" x 8" square and a 2" x 8" strip. Repeat for all of the blocks.

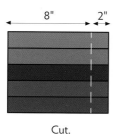

Cut.

3 Sew a pieced 8" square from step 2, a gold-print 2" x 8" strip, and a randomly selected 2" x 8" pieced strip from step 2 together as shown. Rotate the pieced rectangle strip 180° so that the accent pieces within the block do not line up with each other. Press the seam allowances toward the gold accent print, or wait until you arrange the blocks for assembly. You may need to re-press them later so that the seams will butt together. Make 34 blocks.

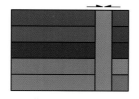

Make 34.

4 Repeat step 3, but rotate the pieced 8" square 90° as shown before sewing it to the gold-print and pieced 2" x 8" strips. Press the seam allowances toward the gold print. Make one block.

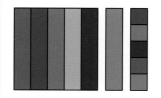

Make 1.

Assembling and Finishing

1 Referring to the quilt assembly diagram, lay out your blocks on a design wall (or other flat surface), in seven rows of five blocks each. (If you left the block seam allowances unpressed, press them to one side after you decide on placement so that they face the opposite direction from the block in the next row or rows.) Sew the blocks together in rows, matching all seam intersections. Pin for accuracy, removing pins as you sew. Press seam allowances in opposite directions from row to row. Sew the rows together, pinning again for accuracy, to complete your quilt top. Press the seam allowances in one direction.

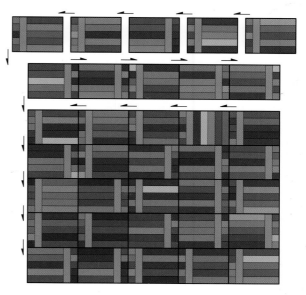

Quilt assembly

2 Referring to "Backing" on page 74, prepare the backing by cutting the fabric into two pieces, approximately 40" x 62". Sew them together along the long edges and trim to make a backing that is 62" square. If you choose to send your top to be quilted by a long-arm machine quilter, check with the quilter for specific requirements regarding backing size. Adjust the backing yardage accordingly.

3 Refer to "Quilt" on page 74 and "Finish" on page 77 for further instructions on quilting options, basting, and binding. Be sure to add a label to your quilt.

HEXAGON SCRAMBLE

Candy wrappers! That's what I see in this quilt. Sometimes it's fun to mix things up. There are times when we're in love with our fabrics. Loooove them! We want to use *all* of them in one quilt. Then we're distracted by a color we never thought we'd add in (for me it was pink). It wasn't part of the specific color scheme I had in mind. But if we think about it, purple, pink, and orange are almost an analogous color scheme, aren't they? Contrast and composition come together to create this design. Well, that and just a little color surprise.

Designed by Natalie Barnes, made by Jane StPierre, quilted by Angela Walters. Fabrics by Alexander Henry Fabrics, Robert Kaufman Fabrics, and Hoffman California Fabrics.

Finished quilt: 51½" x 56½"

Materials

Yardage is based on 42"-wide fabric. Fat quarters are approximately 18" x 21".

9 fat quarters of theme prints for triangle blocks*
5 fat quarters of assorted prints for triangle blocks*
1 yard of accent print for triangle blocks**
⅝ yard of fabric for binding
3½ yards of fabric for backing (consider a print in a
    different scale than the other fabrics)
58" x 63" piece of batting
Template plastic or 60° triangle ruler***

  *Be sure to include one magic color or zinger in your fat
  quarters. See page 15 for additional information.*

  **This accent print will create the hexagon "rings"
  throughout the quilt.*

  ****There are several brands of these rulers on the market.
  I used the Creative Grids 60° Triangle Ruler (CGRT 60),
  which can be used to cut up to 8" finished triangles.*

Cutting

From *each* of the 9 theme prints, cut across the 18" width:
3 strips, 4½" x 18" (27 total)
2 strips, 3½" x 18" (18 total)

From *each* of the 5 assorted prints, cut across the 18" width:
3 strips, 2" x 18" (15 total)
5 strips, 1½" x 18" (25 total)
3 strips, 1" x 18" (15 total)

From the remainder of the assorted prints, cut a *total* of:
3 strips, 3½" x 18"

From the accent print, cut:
21 strips, 1½" x 42"; crosscut into 42 strips,
    1½" x 18"

From the binding fabric, cut:
7 strips, 2¼" x 42"

QUICK CUTTING

Creative Grids makes a ruler that will allow you to cut five 60° triangles at once. If you find you like working with these triangles, you might like to add this tool to your collection of rulers. It's the Creative Grids 60° Double Strip Ruler (CGRDBS 60).

Making the Blocks

1 Sew an accent-print 1½" x 18" strip to each side of a theme- or assorted-print 3½" x 18" strip to make a strip set. Press the seam allowances open. Make 21 strip sets.

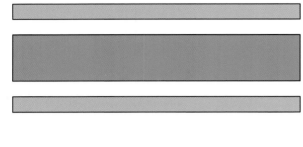

Make 21.

2 If you don't have a 60° triangle ruler, make a triangle template using the pattern on page 38. Using the triangle ruler or template, cut five 4½" triangles from each strip set as shown, for a total of 105. Rotate the ruler or template to cut triangles from both sides of your strips.

Cut 5 from each, 105 total.

3 Carefully remove the small piece of accent fabric from the tip of the triangles and press.

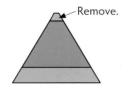 

Remove.

Press.

4 Randomly sew together one assorted 2" x 18" strip, two assorted 1½" x 18" strips, and one assorted 1" x 18" strip. Press the seam allowances open. Make 12 strip sets. (You'll have 7 extra strips.)

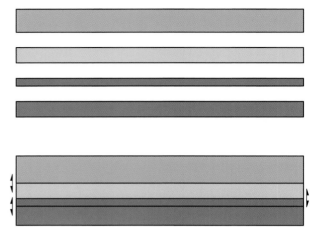
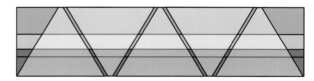

Make 12.

5 Cut a total of 54 triangles, 4½", as you did before using the template or 60° triangle ruler. You can cut extra triangles if you would like to have more options when arranging the triangles on a design wall.

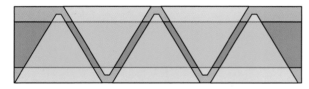

Cut 54 total.

6 Use the triangle ruler or template to cut 135 triangles, 4½", from the theme-print 4½" x 18" strips.

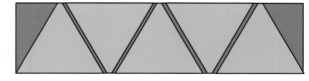

Cut 135 total.

Assembling and Finishing

1 Referring to the quilt assembly diagram, lay out the triangles on a design wall or another available flat surface in 14 rows of 21 triangles each. Group the triangles with accent strips together to create 17 complete hexagons and one half hexagon along the bottom edge. Group the strip-pieced triangles together to create nine hexagons. Arrange them as shown, or as desired.

2 Sew the triangles together in rows. Pin for accuracy, removing pins as you sew. Press all seam allowances open as you sew.

3 Sew the rows together, pinning again for accuracy, to complete your quilt top. Press the seam allowances open.

4 Referring to "Backing" on page 74, prepare the backing by cutting the fabric into two pieces approximately 42" x 62". Sew them together along the long edges and trim to make a backing that is 58" x 63". If you choose to send your top to be quilted by a long-arm machine quilter, check with the quilter for specific requirements regarding backing size. Adjust the backing yardage accordingly.

5 Refer to "Quilt" on page 74 and "Finish" on page 77 for further instructions on quilting options, basting, and binding. Be sure to add a label to your quilt. See also "Binding Hexagons" on page 38.

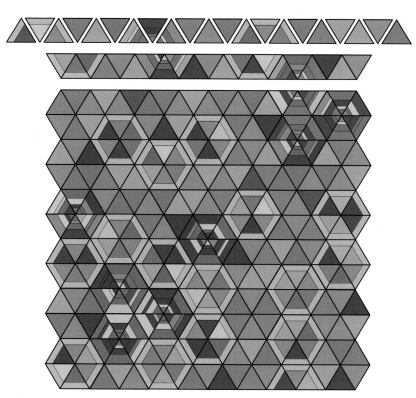

Quilt assembly

BINDING HEXAGONS

For crisp mitered corners when binding the edges of this quilt, follow these simple guidelines.

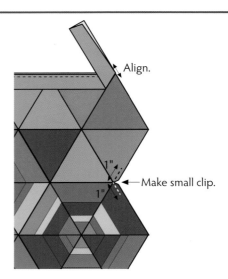

1. Stay stitch each inside angle by stitching a scant ¼" from the quilt-top edge, 1" from each side of the point. Take a small clip at each inner point, taking care not to get too close to the stay stitch.

2. As you attach the binding and reach an inner point, pull down on the quilt just a little to make the angle a little wider, or more open.

3. As you sew toward the outer points, stop at the ¼" point and backstitch. Remove the piece from the machine.

4. Fold the binding up so that the folded edge of the binding and the next raw edge are aligned.

5. Fold the binding down to align the raw edges of the binding and the quilt. Make the fold at the corner.

6. Begin stitching again at the folded edge and continue to sew the binding to the quilt.

When stitching the binding to the back of the quilt, be sure to stitch the miter closed, as you do for regular 90° corners.

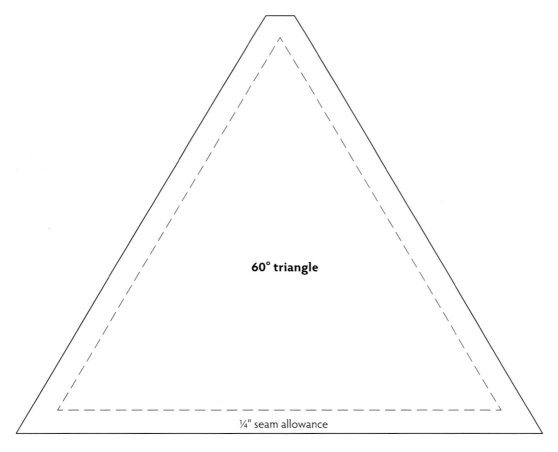

60° triangle

¼" seam allowance

PICNIC TOTE

A woven picnic basket is a thing of beauty. It conjures up romantic images of a basket packed with crystal salt and pepper shakers and the finest of linens and silver. We dream of floating in a rowboat on a lake. But these days, it seems that our lifestyle is more aligned with packing two boxed lunches, putting them in our bag, and biking to the park for a quick getaway. This tote bag, packed with your utensil roll (see page 43), will be ready when you need it.

Designed and made by Natalie Barnes. Fabrics by Windham Fabrics.

Finished bag: 13½" x 10¾" x 2"

Materials

Yardage is based on 42"-wide fabric unless otherwise noted.

⅝ yard of fabric for outside of bag
⅝ yard of fabric for lining and pocket
⅝ yard of fusible fleece (45" wide)

Cutting

See the cutting guide above right before cutting the ⅝-yard pieces.

From *each* fabric, cut:
1 strip, 2" x 42"; trim to 2" x 40"
2 rectangles, 9" x 16"
1 rectangle, 16" x 24"

From the fleece, cut:
1 rectangle, 15½" x 23½"
2 strips, 1½" x 19¾"

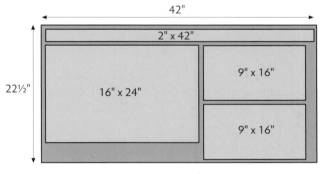

Cutting guide

Making the Tote

1 To make a pocket, layer two matching 9" x 16" rectangles with right sides together. Sew around the perimeter using a ¼" seam allowance; leave a 3" opening for turning. Clip corners and turn the rectangle right side out. Use a wooden chopstick or other blunt tool to push the corners out so they are square. Press. Make two.

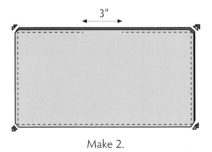

Make 2.

2 Referring to the manufacturer's instructions, fuse the fleece to the wrong side of the 16" x 24" rectangle for the outer bag.

3 Place the pocket made from lining fabric on the right side of the fused outer bag so that it's centered, as shown, 3¾" from the top and bottom, and 4¼" from the sides. Stitch the pocket about ⅛" from the long sides, backstitching at the beginning and ends to reinforce the pocket. Leave the short sides open. Stitch through the center of the pocket for 7¾" to make two pockets on one side, backstitching at the pocket edge. Leave the other side as one large pocket. Add a line of stitching in the other direction through the pocket center, 7¾" from the pocket edges as shown.

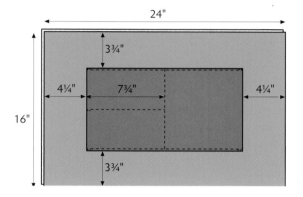

4 Repeat step 3 to sew the pocket made from the outer fabric onto the 16" x 24" lining rectangle.

5 Measure in 11" from the 16" side of the fused outer bag. Begin stitching here and quilt across the bag with a straight line using a walking foot. Stitch across the pocket and repeat to quilt an area that is 2" wide; this will be the bottom of your bag. Quilt each end between the raw edges and the pocket openings in the same manner; this will be the top of your bag.

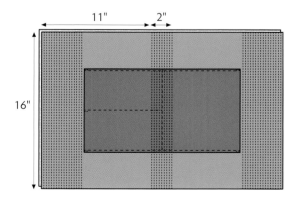

Making the Handles

1 Fuse a 1½" x 19¾" fleece strip to the wrong side of the outer-bag 2" x 40" strip, placing it ¼" away from three edges. Fold the strip in half with right sides together and stitch around the perimeter using a ¼" seam allowance and leaving a 3" opening. Turn the handle right side out and press. Repeat to make a second handle using the strip of lining fabric.

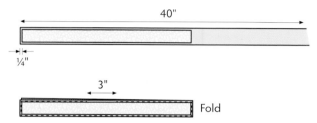

2 Using a walking foot, stitch three or four lines of quilting in the handles.

Assembling and Finishing

1 Measure in 3¾" from each side of the outer bag as shown and pin the handles to the short sides of the bag, aligning the raw edges. The outer edge of the handles should align with the outer pocket edges. Be sure that the handles are flat and not twisted. Baste the handles in place by machine.

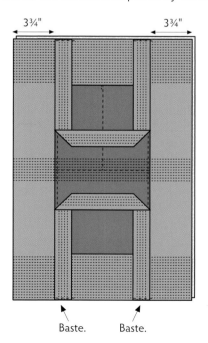

2 Fold the outer bag in half and, with right sides
  facing, stitch the sides of the bag together.
Repeat to stitch the sides of the bag lining, but
leave a 5" opening on one of the sides for turning.

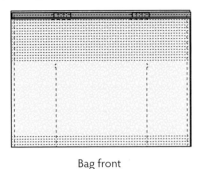

Bag front

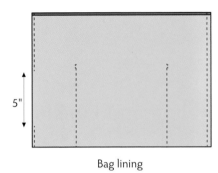

Bag lining

3 Create the bottom of the tote by folding the
  bottom corner of the lining right sides together,
with the side seam centered. Stitch across the fold,
1" from the point, to create a flat bottom. Press.
Repeat on the other side, and then repeat for the
outer bag.

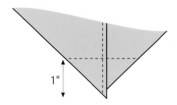

4 Place the bag lining inside the bag front with
  right sides together. Stitch around the top of
the bag.

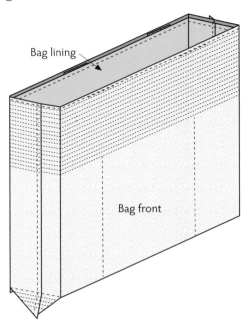

Bag lining

Bag front

5 Turn the bag right side out through the opening
  in the lining. Press and topstitch around the top
of the bag, ¼" from the edges. Sew the opening in
the lining by hand or machine.

PICNIC CASUAL

In my neighborhood, *for six weeks during the summertime, the neighbors all congregate once a week at a nearby park to listen to music by local musicians. Everyone brings a light dinner and sits by the water in beach chairs. The littlest of kids all get up to dance, and the biggest of kids dance, too! It's great to see the grandparents dancing as if no one is looking. These utensil rolls and napkins, along with the tote (page 39), are perfect for an evening in the park, and they will fit in most bike baskets.*

Designed and made by Natalie Barnes. Fabrics by Windham Fabrics.

Finished utensil rolls: 12" x 17"
Finished napkins: 9½" x 9½"

Materials

Materials are for 2 utensil rolls with napkins. Yardage is based on 42"-wide fabric. Fat quarters are approximately 18" x 21".

⅝ yard of light print for pockets and binding
1 fat quarter *each* of 2 accent prints for backing and lining
1 fat quarter of colorful print for napkins
½ yard of dark print for backing and ties
2 pieces of fusible (or regular) batting, 12" x 17"

CHOOSING FABRICS

Sometimes the balance of color, contrast, and composition in a project can be achieved by letting the fabric do the work. For this project, use two different accent prints that will jump off the page just as they are. Choose a background fabric to highlight these fabrics, and you'll have a stunning picnic set.

Cutting

From the dark print, cut:
1 strip, 12" x 42"; crosscut into:
    2 rectangles, 3½" x 12"
    2 rectangles, 11½" x 12"
2 strips, 1" x 42"

From *each* of the accent prints, cut:
1 rectangle, 3½" x 12"
1 rectangle, 12" x 17"

From the light print, cut:
1 strip, 9" x 42"; crosscut into 2 rectangles, 9" x 17"
4 strips, 2¼" x 42"

From the colorful fat quarter, cut:
2 squares*, 10½" x 10½"

It's OK to cut the squares smaller, if your fat quarter is a little scant.

Making the Utensil Rolls

1 Sew a dark-print 11½" x 12" rectangle, an accent-print 3½" x 12" rectangle, and a dark-print 3½" x 12" rectangle together as shown to make a pieced rectangle, 12" x 17", for the back of your utensil roll. Press the seam allowances toward the accent print.

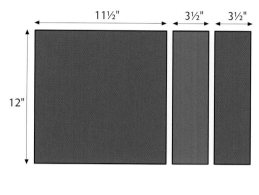

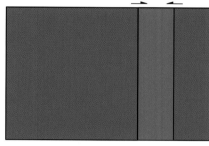

2 Referring to the manufacturer's instructions, fuse the batting between the pieced rectangle from step 1 and the accent-print 12" x 17" rectangle to make a quilt sandwich. If you use regular batting, pin baste the layers together, referring to "Basting" on page 75.

3 Using a walking foot, quilt vertical lines through the layers randomly spaced anywhere from ¼" to 1½" apart.

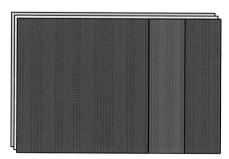

4 Hem the light-print 9" x 17" pocket rectangle by pressing the 17" length of the rectangle under ¼" to the wrong side. Turn under again, and press. Stitch close to the folded edge.

5 Place the hemmed pocket right side up on the accent-print side of the quilted place mat, aligning raw edges along the three sides. Pin in place, and then stitch through the layers at 3" intervals four times to create pockets as shown. Backstitch at the top edge to reinforce the pocket openings.

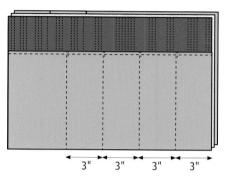

6 To make ties, press the 1" x 42" strips in half lengthwise. Open up each strip, fold both raw edges in to the center fold line, and press again. The strips should now measure ¼" wide. Stitch through the center of each folded strip. Tie each end in a simple knot to finish.

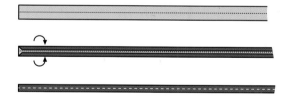

7 Repeat steps 1–6 to make the second utensil roll.

Making the Napkins

1 To hem the small travel napkins, press the edges of the 10½" squares to the wrong side ¼" and then ¼" again.

2 To make the faux mitered corners, open the folds at one corner. With the wrong side up, fold in ¼", and then ¼" again as shown. Press.

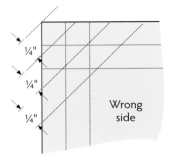
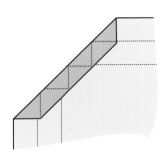

3 Turn the sides of the napkins under again along the folds you made before so that the two edges meet at an angle in the corner. Pin in place. Repeat the process at each corner, and then stitch around the napkin close to the turned-under edge, removing pins as you sew.

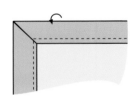

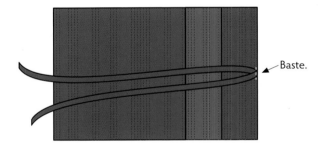

Assembling and Finishing

1 Fold the ties in half and baste one to the backing side of each place mat, in the seam allowance. It should be centered on the 12" side that has the 5"-wide pocket.

Baste.

2 Referring to "Binding" on page 77, bind the utensil rolls with the light-print 2¼" strips. If you like, add your label to the back of one of your utensil rolls. Tuck the napkin into the 5" pocket, and use the rest of the 3" pockets for utensils. Now you have two grab-and-go utensil rolls, with napkins and utensils that are ready whenever you are!

TRIANGLE LINE

If you piece together enough 60° triangles, you're bound to see hexagons eventually. What better way is there to break up that visual image of the hexagon than to incorporate a line? Use either scraps or fat quarters for the triangles, and then select a contrasting accent color for the lines. If you want to create a tribute to the Bauhaus movement, choose neutral colors for the background and red, yellow, and blue for the lines, as shown in the alternate quilt on page 50.

Designed by Natalie Barnes, made by Jane StPierre, quilted by Angela Walters. Fabrics by Hoffman California Fabrics.

Finished quilt: 52½" x 68"

Materials

Yardage is based on 42"-wide fabric. Fat quarters are approximately 18" x 21".

18 fat quarters of assorted light to dark tone on tones for triangle blocks

1 fat quarter of accent color for accent lines*

⅝ yard of fabric for binding

3½ yards of fabric for backing

59" x 74" piece of batting

Template plastic or 60° triangle ruler**

*You'll need 1 fat eighth each of 3 accent colors for the alternate version shown on page 50.

**I used the Creative Grids 60° Triangle Ruler (CGRT 60), but other brands will work too.

Cutting

See "Alternate Cutting for Accent Lines" below if you are using 3 different accent colors as shown on page 50.

From *each* of the 18 fat quarters, cut along the 18" length:

4 strips, 5" x 18" (72 total)

From the accent-color fat quarter, cut:

7 strips, 1½" x 21"; crosscut into:
   13 rectangles, 1½" x 6½"
   8 rectangles, 1½" x 3"

From the binding fabric, cut:

6 strips, 2¼" x 42"

ALTERNATE CUTTING FOR ACCENT LINES

From blue fabric, cut:
3 rectangles, 1½" x 6½"
2 rectangles, 1½" x 3"

From yellow fabric, cut:
2 rectangles, 1½" x 6½"
1 rectangle, 1½" x 3"

From red fabric, cut:
8 rectangles, 1½" x 6½"
5 rectangles, 1½" x 3"

Making the Blocks

1. Using a 60° triangle ruler or templates made from the patterns on page 51, crosscut each of the 5" strips into four 60° triangles for a total of 288 triangles (3 are extra). Rotate the ruler or template to make continuous cuts. Cut a total of 15 left-facing half triangles and 15 right-facing half triangles from the ends of the strips.

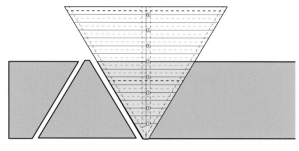

Cut 285.

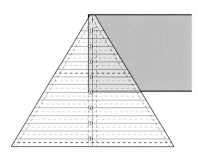

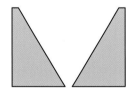

Cut 15 of each.

2. Select 13 of the 60° triangles and trim 1" off the bottom. Select eight of the triangles and trim 1" off the flattened tip of the triangles

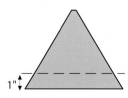

Trim 13.

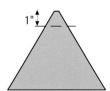

Trim 8.

3. Sew an accent 1½" x 6½" rectangle to the bottom of the 13 triangles from step 2. Sew an accent 1½" x 3" rectangle to the top of each of the eight triangles. Trim the excess fabric to align with the triangle edges.

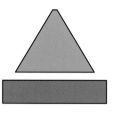

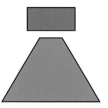

Make 13.

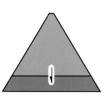

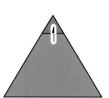

Make 8.

PIECING POINTER

Keep those points along the bottom of your triangles intact. (Some quilters refer to these as "dog ears.") These points will be your friend when sewing 60° triangles to each other.

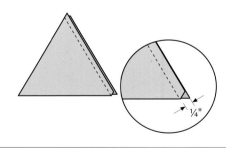

This version of "Triangle Line" features light neutrals for the triangles. Designed by Natalie Barnes, made by Jane StPierre, quilted by Angela Walters. Fabrics by Dear Stella Design and from Natalie's stash.

Assembling and Finishing

1 Referring to the quilt assembly diagram on page 51, begin placing the triangles on a design wall in 15 horizontal rows of 19 triangles each. Include a half triangle on each end of the rows. Spend some time arranging the different fabrics. Step away from your project for a while, or "sleep on it." Take another look at your layout, revising those areas where the same colors or prints are bunched together. Move the fabrics around until you are pleased with the layout.

2 Remove one row from the design wall, left to right, stacking pieces with the left-end triangle on the top and the right-end triangle on the bottom. Place this stack by your sewing machine, and begin joining triangles by sewing the first two pieces on the top of the pile together. Align the half-triangle right sides together and sew the seam. Finger-press the seam allowances open, or press them open with your iron. Continue to add triangles until the row is complete.

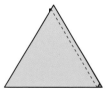 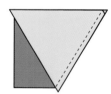

3 Return the row to the design wall and continue to piece the remaining rows.

4 Remove the first two rows from the design wall and pin them right sides together carefully to match the triangle points; sew the rows together. Take a look at the points. Don't they look lovely? You

did it! Press the seam allowances open. Continue sewing your rows together until your quilt top is complete.

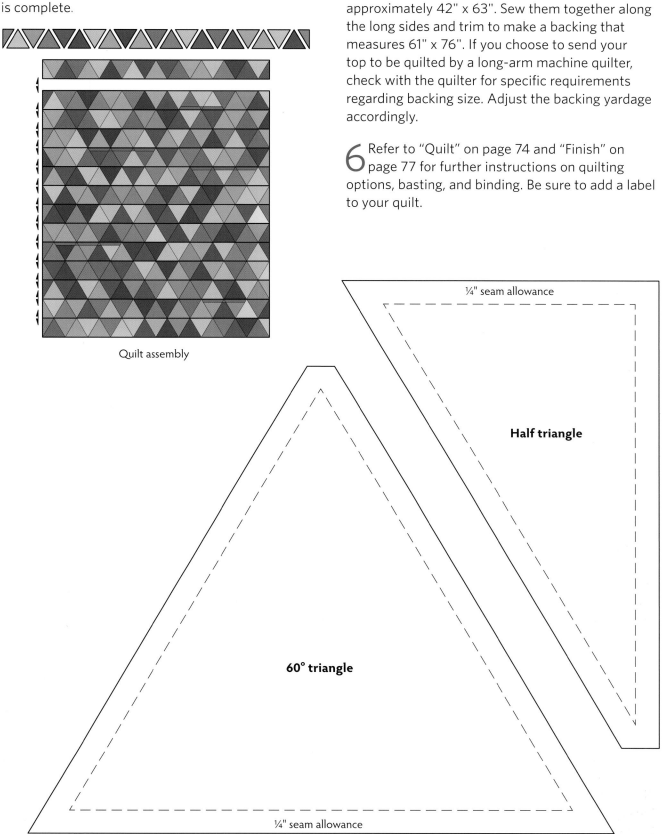

Quilt assembly

5 Referring to "Backing" on page 74, prepare the backing by cutting the fabric into two pieces approximately 42" x 63". Sew them together along the long sides and trim to make a backing that measures 61" x 76". If you choose to send your top to be quilted by a long-arm machine quilter, check with the quilter for specific requirements regarding backing size. Adjust the backing yardage accordingly.

6 Refer to "Quilt" on page 74 and "Finish" on page 77 for further instructions on quilting options, basting, and binding. Be sure to add a label to your quilt.

¼" seam allowance

Half triangle

60° triangle

¼" seam allowance

COMPOSITION

There is no work of art without a system.

—Le Corbusier

Every endeavor has an organizing element. It isn't just limited to the arts. Cooking has its own math and science. Even quilting has what we commonly refer to as "quilting math." If you delve into the world of graphic design, you will inevitably run into the concept of the typographic grid, an organizing principle of graphic design.

Origins of Composition

If you look into the world of twentieth-century design, including the Bauhaus school of design and the works of Kandinsky, Klee, Mies van der Rohe, Walter Gropius, or Le Corbusier, you will find the foundation of modern design that seems to have a resurgence in today's aesthetic.

Finally, if you speak with a mathematician, you will learn that all form is derived from ratios. And these ratios are ever defined for us in nature and beauty.

"I just want to make a quilt," you say to yourself. But I suggest, before you make that quilt, you take a moment to look at the amount of each color you're going to put into that quilt. Consider the placement of each color in your quilt top. What shapes will you use in your quilt top? Squares? Rectangles? What will the proportions of those shapes be?

Ancient Greek mathematicians gave us the golden ratio, or golden section that we know today. Fibonacci gave us divine proportion, a numeric sequence for it.

Look at the interior of a nautilus shell. Take a look at the spiral pattern of a sunflower. The ratio? Phi, or 1 to 1.68. Pinecones, and even the positioning of leaves on a stalk, are in divine proportion.

Da Vinci created the Vitruvian man to explain proportion. Le Corbusier called his proportional system Le Modulor. And all of these scales were put to use to make decisions about the scale used in art and architecture.

I think what all of these theories are really trying to say is this: We have evolved our sciences to explain our aesthetic. We understand what perfect pitch in music is and why it sounds better to us than the alternative. While there may be a theory to why we like the traditional layout of our quilt blocks, we like the order and the predictability of the layout that we can describe.

A Modern Aesthetic

There is a more modern aesthetic among some quilters, and a new preference, on occasion, for something other than the predictable grid system of design. We want to use a rectangle instead of a square for our blocks. We want to combine squares and rectangles and strips in our composition. We want more surprise and less predictability. Many of today's quilt designs also feature a minimalistic approach.

Let's use good tools to work toward a modern aesthetic. Let's apply some math to our decisions about what size rectangle we're going to use. Let's place the accents in our quilt tops in accordance with the Vetruvian man or Le Modulor. If science and math and the arts tell us that these are the "pleasing aesthetics" of nature, let's incorporate them into our quilts.

These concepts may intrigue you, and you may delight a mathematician with the design of your next quilt top or wall hanging. You may think twice, and get out a calculator the next time you want to convert a typical square block design into a rectangle. And the next time you see a sunflower, you will marvel at the pattern made by the seeds.

Contrast and Comparison

When I made the first version of the table runner "Ranch String" (page 54), I was house sitting on a cattle ranch on the coast of California. In the morning, I would go out to the garden for breakfast and pick fresh strawberries, still cold from the nighttime's chill. I would stand and watch as the coyotes headed up the mountain and back into the canyons after a night of hunting.

"Ranch String" in the workshop.
PHOTOGRAPHY: NATALIE BARNES

I spent my days in work boots, jeans, T-shirts, and an old barn jacket, weeding, watering, and worrying. Would the snake in the berry bramble find the nest of baby birds? Would the seedlings in the hothouse grow strong enough to transplant?

When the shadows would grow long on the day, I would head to my room over the workshop and sew. It was a lesson in contrast and comparison, creating beautiful textiles among the tractors and the tools.

In the seemingly chaotic bramble of a garden of berries and veggies and taro and radishes and colorful kale, there is order. And in the seemingly chaotic rhythm of ranching, there is a season to everything. Standing shoulder to shoulder with someone, trying to help a cow birth a calf and seeing that calf finally gasp its first breath is a wonder. But in all of this ranch life, there must be order.

Every time I make a block with a strong organizing fabric, or focus fabric, I think of the strength it takes to be a rancher. It is a romantic idea, the wilds of the West. But the reality of it is this: one must have order, or one will end up with chaos.

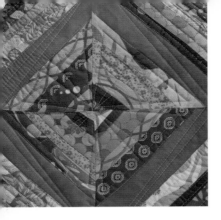

RANCH STRING

String quilts have been stitched as make-do, use-it-up quilts for hundreds of years. They have historically been utilitarian quilts made from whatever scraps were available, usually strips or "strings" left over from other projects or from worn-out clothing. Instead of throwing something away during hard times, a resourceful quiltmaker would put it to use. Many antique string-quilt blocks were stitched onto old newspapers for stability. It is the romance of sitting down with a pile of scraps and making something from seemingly nothing that appeals to me.

Designed and made by Natalie Barnes, quilted by Angela Walters. Fabrics from Natalie's stash (Andover, Windham Fabrics, and additional scrap fabrics by Denyse Schmidt and Anna Maria Horner).

Finished table runner: 13½" x 104½"
Finished block: 6½" x 6½"

Materials

Yardage is based on 42"-wide fabric.

3 yards *total* of assorted scraps for blocks
1¼ yards of accent fabric for blocks and binding
1⅝ yards of fabric for backing
20" x 111" piece of batting
Paper for foundation piecing

Cutting

From the accent fabric, cut:
4 rectangles, 10½" x 18"; crosscut into 32 strips,
    2" x 10½"
7 strips, 2¼" x 42"

From the assorted scraps, cut:
150 strips, 1½" x 9"
150 strips, 1" x 9"

From the foundation paper, cut:
32 squares, 7" x 7"

MIX IT UP

While you can always use fat quarters and fat eighths, think of this project as a challenge to use your stash. Pull all of the fabrics from your scrap boxes as you sew. Include ugly and magic colors (see page 15). Put some unexpected colors in your blocks. Consider adding a Civil War–reproduction print or a 1970s-looking calico print. Mix up the scale of prints. You might even include some woven plaids or a shot cotton. What about an old linen tea towel? Linen calendar towels are fun to cut up and use in quilts. If you have a favorite multicolored print you'd like to use, look at the color windows or dots on the selvages to help you choose other fabrics. In short, mix things up and have fun doing it! Your project will be a real conversation piece at the dinner table.

Making the Blocks

By using your accent fabric in the same place—the diagonal center of the block—you'll be making blocks that you can then arrange to make a secondary pattern. For the quilt shown in the photograph, the blocks were arranged to create a simple diamond. Before stitching the blocks together, take some time to try different layouts. Turn them and see what other designs you can make from this simple utilitarian block.

1 Place a 2" x 10½" strip of accent fabric right side up on your 7" square of foundation paper, positioning it on the diagonal from corner to corner. The strips will be longer than needed; you'll trim the ends even with the paper after you have covered the foundation with strips.

2 Choose a 9"-long strip from the assorted strips and place it right sides together with the accent fabric strip, aligning the raw edges. Sew together with a ¼" seam allowance through all layers. Flip open and finger-press the seam allowances, or press with an iron.

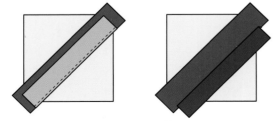

3 Repeat step 2 to add additional strips to each side of the accent strip, varying the strip widths and colors, until the entire 7" x 7" piece is covered. Trim your "strings" to shorter lengths as you approach the corners of the 7"-square foundation.

4 Repeat steps 1–3 until all 32 foundation squares have been covered with fabric strips.

Make 32.

5 Trim the blocks so that the strips are even with the 7"-square foundation. With right side up, press the blocks using spray sizing or spray starch. Note that if you use starch, be sure to wash your project once it's completed.

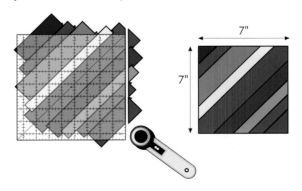

Assembling and Finishing

1 Refer to the quilt assembly diagram at right and arrange the blocks on a design wall or other flat surface, in 16 rows of two blocks each. Sew the blocks together in rows. Pin for accuracy, removing pins as you sew. Press the seam allowances in opposite directions from row to row. Sew the rows together, matching the block seam allowances and pinning for accuracy, to complete your quilt top. Press the remaining seam allowances in one direction.

2 Stitch around the perimeter of the top a scant ¼" from the raw edges to keep seam allowances from coming unsewn and to prevent stretching or distortion of the blocks. The edges of the blocks are all cut on the bias and will stretch easily, so handle the top gently. Carefully remove the papers from the back of the blocks.

3 Referring to "Backing" on page 74, prepare the backing by cutting the fabric into two pieces approximately 21" x 56". Sew them together to make a backing that measures 21" x 112". If you choose to send your top to be quilted by a long-arm machine quilter, check with the quilter for specific requirements regarding backing size. Adjust the backing yardage accordingly.

4 Refer to "Quilt" on page 74 and "Finish" on page 77 for further instructions on quilting options, basting, and binding. Be sure to add a label to your quilt. This is a table runner that will blend with any table setting you choose!

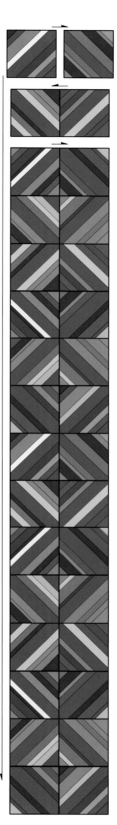

Quilt assembly

CIRCLE SHUFFLE

This quilt is surprisingly simple. You will make nine 24"-square blocks, using the three light prints for the background and varying only the colors for the reverse appliqué pieces. Then rotate the simple blocks to create a much more complex-looking design. Your friends will think you took a lot of time arranging the circles— little will they know! When this quilt is made in whites and happy polka dots, I think of a child's room or a backyard filled with balls. Now paint this picture in your mind: the background is made from medium grays and olive greens, while the circles are filled with creams and khakis and soft golds. The random circles have just become a modern twist.

Designed by Natalie Barnes, made by Jane StPierre, quilted by Angela Walters. Fabrics by Dear Stella Design.

Finished quilt: 72½" x 72½"
Finished block: 24" x 24"

Materials

Yardage is based on 42"-wide fabric. Fat quarters are approximately 18" x 21".

27 fat quarters of colorful prints for circles
1⅝ yards *each* of 3 light prints for background
⅝ yard of fabric for binding
4½ yards of fabric for backing
78" x 78" piece of batting
Template plastic or Easy Circle Cut Ruler by Sharon Hultgren
Pearl cotton thread in bright colors for appliqué (optional)
Embroidery needle for pearl cotton

Cutting

From *each* of the 3 light prints, cut:
3 strips, 12½" x 42"; crosscut *each* strip into:
　　3 rectangles, 9½" x 12½" (9 from each print, 27 total)
　　3 rectangles, 3½" x 12½" (9 from each print, 27 total)
2 strips, 6½" x 42"; crosscut into 12 squares, 6½" x 6½" (36 total)

From *each* of the 27 colorful-print fat quarters, cut:
1 rectangle, 12" x 21"; crosscut into:
　　1 rectangle, 9" x 12" (27 total)
　　1 rectangle, 3" x 12" (27 total)

From *each of 9* of the colorful-print fat quarters, cut:
1 square, 6" x 6" (9 total)

From the binding fabric, cut:
8 strips, 2¼" x 42"

Making the Blocks

1 Randomly select different light-print 3½" x 12½" and 9½" x 12½" rectangles and sew them together in pairs. Press the seam allowances open. Make 27.

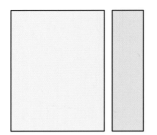 

Make 27.

2 Select two matching pairs of light-print 6½" squares and sew them together into a four-patch unit as shown. Press the seam allowances open. Make nine four-patch units.

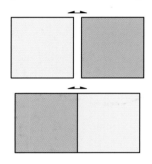

Make 9.

3 Using a design wall or other flat surface, arrange three of the units from step 1 and one four-patch unit from step 2 as shown. Once you're pleased with the placement of fabrics, sew the four units together to make the 24½"-square block. Make a total of nine blocks.

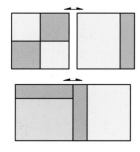

Make 9.

4 Randomly select different colorful-print 9" x 12" and 3" x 12" rectangles and sew them together in pairs as shown. Press the seam allowances open. Make 27.

Make 27.

5 Place a unit from step 4 behind one of the background blocks, aligning the seams with one quadrant of the block. The right side of the colorful block should face the wrong side of the background. Baste into place around the outer edges by machine. Repeat for the other two large quadrants. Center one colorful 6" square behind the center-most square of the four-patch unit and baste it in place.

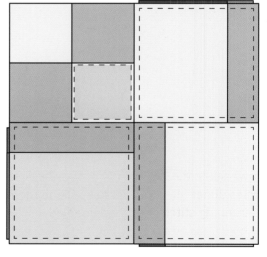

Baste.

6 Make circle templates using the patterns on page 62 or use your circle ruler. With a pencil, draw a 4"-diameter circle in the center of the designated 6" square and draw a 10"-diameter circle in the center of each of the three remaining quadrants of the block. Carefully cut out the circles on the drawn lines.

7 Make small clips about ³⁄₁₆" into the seam allowance of the circles. Turn the raw edges of the circles under ¼" and reverse appliqué them by using a running stitch near the folded edges. Let the running stitch show; I used pearl cotton and an embroidery needle.

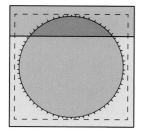 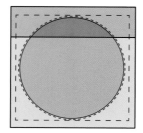

8 Remove the basting stitches and trim the excess fabric from the wrong side, leaving ¼" beyond the stitching.

Assembling and Finishing

1 Referring to the quilt assembly diagram on page 62, arrange the blocks on a design wall or other flat surface in three rows of three blocks each. Rotate them as shown. Sew the blocks together in rows, matching all seam intersections. Pin for accuracy, removing pins as you sew. Press the seam allowances in opposite directions from row to row. Sew the rows together, pinning again for accuracy, to complete your quilt top. Press the seam allowances in one direction.

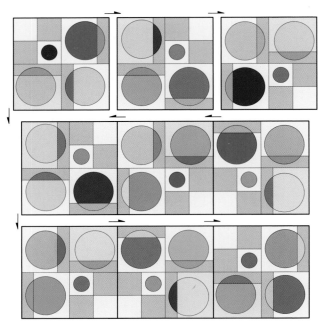

Quilt assembly

2 Referring to "Backing" on page 74, prepare the backing by cutting the fabric into two pieces approximately 42" x 83". Sew them together along the long edges and trim to make a backing that measures 78" x 78". If you choose to send your top to be quilted by a long-arm machine quilter, check with the quilter for specific requirements regarding backing size. Adjust the backing yardage accordingly.

3 Refer to "Quilt" on page 74 and "Finish" on page 77 for further instructions on quilting options, basting, and binding. Be sure to add a label to your quilt, "Made with love!"

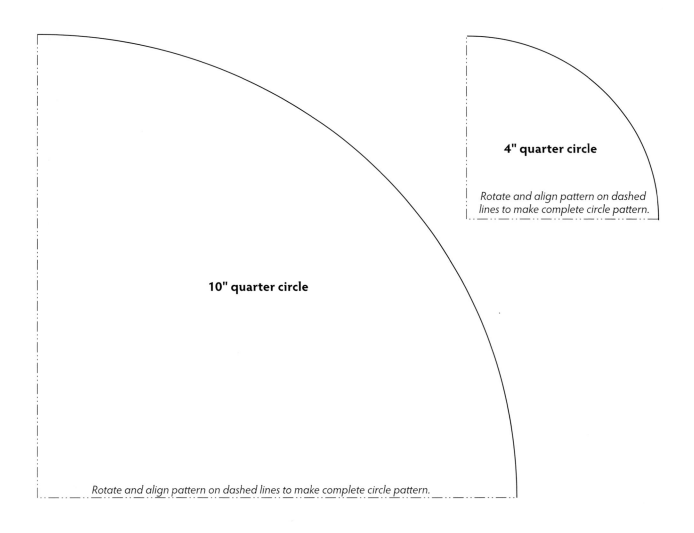

4" quarter circle

Rotate and align pattern on dashed lines to make complete circle pattern.

10" quarter circle

Rotate and align pattern on dashed lines to make complete circle pattern.

SQUARE TUMBLE

My favorite way to set a table for four is with two table runners, using the runners for the place settings. The runners don't have to be identical, but they should be similar. In the runners shown, I just mixed up the random layout of the blocks. These are simple to make, and the larger pieces in the runners will showcase your favorite accent fabrics.

Designed and made by Natalie Barnes, quilted by Angela Walters. Fabrics by Robert Kaufman Fabrics.

Finished runners: 15½" x 93½"
Finished block: 15" x 15"

Materials

Materials are for 2 runners. Yardage is based on 42"-wide fabric. Fat quarters are approximately 18" x 21".

8 to 10 fat quarters in assorted neutrals for blocks
3 fat quarters of accent prints #1–#3 for block rectangles
1 fat quarter of accent print #4 for block squares and sashing strips
1 yard of fabric for binding
2¾ yards of fabric for backing
2 pieces, 21" x 99", of batting

Cutting

From the 8 to 10 assorted neutrals, cut *a total of*:
240 squares, 3½" x 3½"

From *each* of accent prints #1–#3, cut:
4 rectangles, 3½" x 15½" (12 total)

From accent print #4, cut:
3 strips, 3½" x 18"; crosscut into 12 squares, 3½" x 3½"
6 strips, 1½" x 18"; crosscut into 6 strips, 1½" x 15½"

From the binding fabric, cut:
12 strips, 2¼" x 42"

Making the Blocks

1 Randomly select five assorted neutral 3½" squares and sew them together to make a strip measuring 3½" x 15½". Press the seam allowances in one direction. Make 36.

Make 36.

2 Randomly select four assorted neutral 3½" squares and sew them together with one accent #4 square as shown to make a strip measuring 3½" x 15½". Press the seam allowances in one direction. Make 12.

Make 12.

3 Arrange and sew three units from step 1, one unit from step 2, and one accent 3½" x 15½" rectangle as shown. Make eight of block A, two of block B, and two of block C.

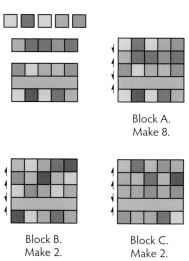

Block A.
Make 8.

Block B.
Make 2.

Block C.
Make 2.

Assembling and Finishing

1 Referring to the quilt assembly diagrams below, arrange the six blocks and three of the accent 1½" x 15½" strips on your design wall. Move the strips around and rotate the blocks until you are pleased with your layout and there is variation in the placement of the fabrics.

2 Remove the pieces from your design wall and stack them top to bottom, in the order in which you will sew them. As a precaution, place a pin through the blocks before carrying them to your machine. Sew the blocks and accent strips together. Press the seam allowances in one direction.

3 Repeat steps 1 and 2 to assemble the second table runner.

4 Referring to "Backing" on page 74, prepare the backing by cutting the fabric into two pieces approximately 21" x 99". If you choose to send your top to be quilted by a long-arm machine quilter, check with the quilter for specific requirements regarding backing size. Adjust the backing yardage accordingly.

5 Refer to "Quilt" on page 74 and "Finish" on page 77 for further instructions on quilting options, basting, and binding. Be sure to add a label to your table runners.

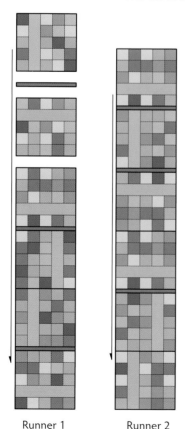

Runner 1   Runner 2

Quilt assembly

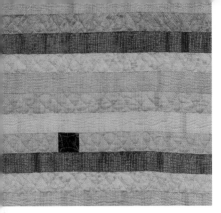

RESTING LINE

Architects and industrial designers have used the phrase "form follows function" for a long time. That saying was the watchword for the design of this quilt. Design something neutral. Design something colorful. Design something with a color scheme that will blend with whatever sheets are on the bed. Design something restful. And make it big enough to cover a queen-size bed.

Designed and made by Natalie Barnes, quilted by Angela Walters. Fabrics by Robert Kaufman Fabrics.

Finished quilt: 83½" x 84½"

Materials

Yardage is based on 42"-wide fabric. Fat quarters are approximately 18" x 21".

1⅓ yards *each* of 3 light neutral fabrics for background*

7 fat quarters of assorted prints for left column

6 fat quarters of assorted prints for right column

1 fat quarter of accent fabric for squares

¾ yard of fabric for binding

7⅝ yards of fabric for backing

90" x 91" piece of batting

*If any of your fabrics are less than 42" wide after removing the selvages, you can still use them. Simply make the middle section (C) slightly narrower.

TWO FOR ONE

Select a backing fabric that you'll enjoy, and you can use both sides of the quilt. Choose contrasting binding so that when you use the reverse side of your quilt on the bed, you will still have an accent.

Cutting

From *each* of the 3 light neutral fabrics, cut:
10 strips, 4" x 42" (30 total; 1 is extra). From the strips, crosscut:
> 5 strips into 5 strips, 4" x 38½"
> 5 strips into 24 rectangles, 4" x 7½"

From *each* of the 7 fat quarters for the left column, cut:
8 strips, 2" x 21" (56 total). From the strips, crosscut:
> 6 strips into 6 strips, 2" x 13¼", and
> > 6 rectangles, 2" x 6¾"
> 6 strips into 6 strips, 2" x 19½"

From *each* of the 6 fat quarters for the right column, cut:
1 strip, 2" x 21" (6 total)

From the *remainder* of the 6 fat quarters, cut *a total of*:
53 strips, 2" x 14½" (2 are extra)*
7 strips, 2" x 13" (2 are extra)*

From the accent fat quarter, cut:
1 strip, 4" x 21"; crosscut into 5 squares, 4" x 4"
2 strips, 2" x 21"; crosscut into 17 squares, 2" x 2"

From the binding fabric, cut:
9 strips, 2¼" x 42"

*Cut these strips across the 16" length.

Making the Blocks

1 Sew an accent 2" square to a 2" x 19½" strip to form a 2" x 21" strip. Press the seam allowances toward the square. Make six.

Make 6.

2 Sew an accent 2" square, a 2" x 13¼" strip, and a 2" x 6¾" rectangle together as shown to form a 2" x 21" strip. Press the seam allowances toward the square. Make six.

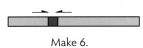

Make 6.

3 Sew one strip from step 1 and one strip from step 2 together with three 2" x 21" strips as shown to make a block. Press the seam allowances in one direction. Make six of these blocks for section B.

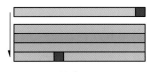

Make 6.

4 Sew an accent 4" square to a neutral 4" x 38½" strip. Press the seam allowances toward the accent square. Make five for section C.

Make 5.

5 Sew an accent 2" square to a 2" x 13" strip to form a 2" x 14½" strip. Press the seam allowances toward the square. Make five for section D.

Make 5.

Making the Sections

Refer to the quilt assembly diagram on page 69 for these steps.

1 Sew 24 neutral 4" x 7½" rectangles together to make section A. Press the seam allowances toward what will be the bottom of the column.

2 To make section B, select 26 strips, 2" x 21", and sew them together randomly with the blocks from step 3 of "Making the Blocks." Mix in a few of the strips cut from the right-column fabrics. Press the seam allowances toward the top.

3 Sew the five strips from step 4 of "Making the Blocks" together randomly with 19 neutral 4" x 42" strips to make section C. Press the seam allowances downward.

4 To make section D, select 51 strips, 2" x 14½", and sew them together randomly with the five units from step 5 of "Making the Blocks." Press the seam allowances upward.

KEEP IT STRAIGHT

While sewing long strips together, alternate the sewing direction from strip to strip. Pin along the length of the pieces you are sewing, matching the ends. This will ensure that the strips remain straight and square.

Assembling and Finishing

1 Referring to the quilt assembly diagram, sew sections A and B together and sections C and D together. Note that seven of the 1½"-wide strips will equal three of the 3½"-wide strips. Pin at these seams, and at the top and bottom of each section. You may need to re-press some of the seam allowances so they butt together. Remove pins as you sew the sections together. Press seam allowances toward section A and section C.

2 Pin section A/B to C/D. Place the bulk of the top in your lap. Begin sewing, removing pins as you stitch. As you sew, place the quilt top on your

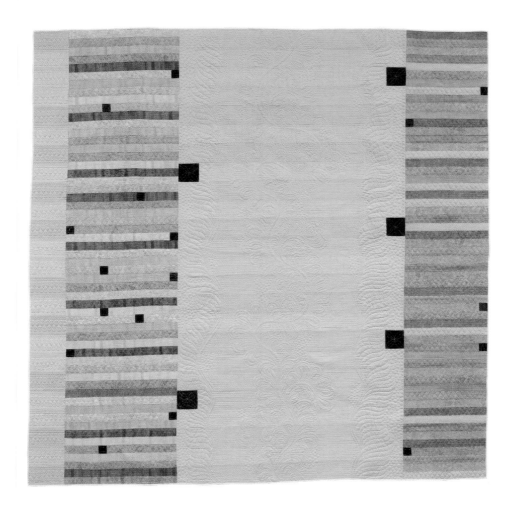

sewing table, to the left of your machine, so the weight of the top does not pull on your seam as you sew the final pieces together. Press the seam allowances toward section C.

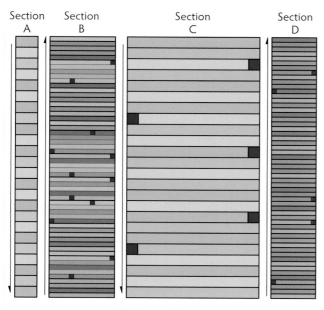

Quilt assembly

3 Referring to "Backing" on page 74, prepare the backing by cutting it into three pieces approximately 42" x 91". Sew them together along the long edges and trim to make a backing that measures 90" x 91". If you choose to send your top to be quilted by a long-arm machine quilter, check with the quilter for specific requirements regarding backing size. Adjust the backing yardage accordingly. Be sure to discuss batting options with your long-arm quilter, as well. Remember, this will be used as a quilt on your bed. Select a batting that will give you the desired warmth and a weight that you're comfortable with.

4 Refer to "Quilt" on page 74 and "Finish" on page 77 for further instructions on quilting options, basting, and binding. Be sure to add a label to your quilt. You now have something that is designed for function!

Cut + Piece + Quilt + Finish

The thing I love most about quilting is that it can be done with the most basic of tools and supplies. I remember when I made my very first quilt—I drafted a pattern onto a paper bag. I traced the pieces onto cardboard and cut the templates with metal dressmaker shears. I placed those templates on my fabrics, traced around them with a ballpoint pen, and cut the pieces with the same scissors I used to cut the cardboard templates. I used my mother's portable Singer sewing machine to piece the quilt top, and, well, once I saw how the fabrics and shapes came together to make that geometric design, I was hooked!

Years later I was returning from a quilt show with a group of friends. We were traveling by train, so we had a little free time on our hands. I was so excited about a new pattern I had just purchased at the show, that I cut up the appliqué pattern, pinned it to some fabric in my shopping bag, cut it out, and with a little needle and thread, began to appliqué my project."You can't do that!" one of my friends exclaimed. "Why not?" I asked. "Well," she replied, "you just can't. It won't turn out right!" A year later, that quilt hung in our local guild show. I don't think anyone was the wiser about my enthusiastic technique. Yes, you should use your "best practices," but you should also be really excited about the process. Have a passion for your projects, and celebrate your own unique approach to quilting!

Today, we have so many tools to choose from that help us get through the process more quickly and more accurately. But in reality, if you wanted to start quilting tomorrow, what you would need, in the simplest of terms, would be fabric, scissors, a needle and thread, and an idea. I love that about quilting.

In this section, I have listed a few of my favorite tools and techniques. If you are left-handed, try to shop for non-handed tools. I encourage you to take a class at your local quilt shop, at a conference, or through your quilt guild. There is also more

Assorted tools and supplies used in quiltmaking

DESIGN WALL

Find a place in your sewing studio or your home where you can vertically hang or install a design wall. It can be as simple as a piece of batting, flannel, or felt on a flat surface. Audition or "interview" your fabrics by putting them up on your design wall. Stepping back from your work will help you make better color and value placement decisions. Arrange your blocks on the design wall before assembling your quilt, so you can be sure your eye isn't drawn to one particular area of your project.

detailed information at ShopMartingale.com and on many of the manufacturers' websites listed under "Resources" (page 79).

Be sure you have the proper tools to create something that will be your legacy. It's so much easier to make quilts more quickly these days with the tools and resources that are available to us. But remember, what you make may last more than a lifetime.

Cut

Most of today's quilt patches are cut with rotary cutters, but you'll also want scissors for various cutting tasks. Here's what you'll need.

Rotary cutter. A 45 mm cutter is perfect for everyday cutting of strips and blocks; a 28 mm cutter is handy for detail work and precise trimming. Place cutters in a box, away from unskilled users, children, and pets.

Scissors. Use 8" dressmaker shears for cutting fabrics, stabilizers, and fusible web; use smaller scissors or clippers for handwork or detailed trimming.

Acrylic rulers. You'll want a variety of ruler sizes on hand for different tasks.

6" x 24" or 6½" x 24" for cutting strips
6½" x 12½" for crosscuts
12" x 12" for squaring up blocks
4½" x 4½" for trimming
60° triangle ruler
30° triangle ruler

Cutting mat. A 24" x 36" self-healing cutting mat is the most versatile size to have. An additional cutting mat placed adjacent to your sewing machine is handy for trimming and small cuts.

To rotary cut, follow these steps:

1 Press your fabrics before you begin cutting. Square up the fabric by aligning your 6" x 24" ruler with a smaller 6" x 12" or 6" square ruler that is aligned with the fold of your fabric. Remove the smaller ruler, holding the long ruler in place with your non-cutting hand. With your dominant hand, place the edge of the rotary cutter against the acrylic ruler and carefully roll the cutter away from you. Remember to close the rotary-cutting

blade after every cut. It is "good practice" and prevents accidents.

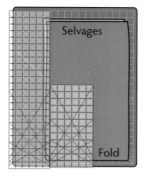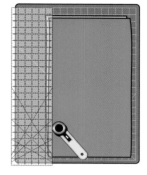

Align a mark on the smaller ruler's edge with the fold.

Cut along long ruler's edge.

2 With the squared-up edge to your left, and your ruler to your left, you're ready to cut strips. To cut, for example, a 2½" strip, place the 2½" mark of the ruler on the squared-up edge of the fabric and align the folded edge of the fabric with a horizontal mark on your ruler to be sure you are cutting perpendicular to the fold. Always use your ruler to measure, rather than the cutting mat. Remember, measure left, and cut right.

Align mark on the ruler (2½")
with fabric edge.

3 Many patterns will require you to cut strips and then crosscut those strips into smaller pieces. After cutting the strip, trim off the selvage or woven edges of the fabric strip using a ruler and rotary cutter. Then rotate the cutting mat 180° as shown on page 72. Using a smaller acrylic ruler, align the straight edge of the fabric on the left with the required measurement on the ruler, and cut

from the right. Continue cutting until you have the correct number of pieces for your project.

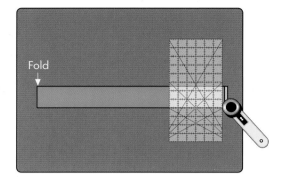

Trim selvage edges.

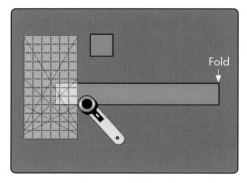

Rotate the mat and place a line on the ruler on the edge of the strip.

4 Sometimes a pattern will require you to crosscut strips of fabric that are sewn together into a strip set. Square up one edge of the strip set, and crosscut by aligning the edge of the fabric with the required measurement. You should also align one of the pieced seams with a horizontal mark on your ruler to be sure you are cutting perpendicular to the seam, as well.

CUT WIDE TO NARROW FOR LONG STRIPS

When cutting long, narrow strips, I cut a wider strip to be sure my fabric is perpendicular to the fold, and then cut the smaller strips from that piece. As an example, it's difficult to be sure a 1" strip is square. If a pattern calls for four strips, 1" x 21", I will cut one piece 4" x 21" and then cut my 1" strips from that larger piece.

Piece

Unless you are hand piecing, you'll need a sewing machine. Use a straight stitch set at a length of 12 to 15 stitches per inch. All of my quilt tops are pieced on a 1980s industrial Bernina sewing machine. When away from home, I use a 1940s metal straight-stitch Singer sewing machine or an even older Singer Featherweight. Find a machine that speaks to you. You will use it often and may one day pass it on to someone in your family.

In addition to a sewing machine and its manual, you'll need the following items for machine piecing:

Machine needles. Universal needles work well for piecing quilting cottons.

Thread. I use 50-weight, long-staple cotton thread. Using a fine, thin thread means less bulk in the seams, which will improve your accuracy. Using a long-staple cotton will also reduce the lint in your machine.

Pins. Select long, thin straight pins with heads that you can easily grab.

Seam ripper. This tool lives just to the right of my machine. I cut threads with it, instead of using scissors or clippers. By cutting my threads this way, I am assured I won't cut a hole in something. I also use it as a stiletto, to keep my fingers away from the needle of my machine. And, yes, I do rip seams with it as well. I lay my sewn piece flat, insert the tip of the seam ripper into every third stitch, and cut the thread. I then turn the piece over and pull the thread on the other side. As I always say in class, "Never rip a seam when you're still mad at yourself for sewing it incorrectly."

FIND YOUR ACCURATE ¼" SEAM ALLOWANCE

Machine piecing a quilt top requires sewing using an accurate ¼" seam allowance. Even if you have a ¼" presser foot for your machine, test for accuracy. Cut three strips, 1½" x 4", and sew them together with a ¼" seam allowance. Press and measure your piece. It should measure exactly 3½". If not, take a ruler to your machine. Put the needle down on your ruler's ¼" line. Put a piece of painter's tape on your machine, aligning it with the right edge of the ruler. Sew another set of strips and measure again. Reposition the tape until you have an exact ¼" seam allowance.

CHAIN PIECE

To sew efficiently, use an assembly-line technique. Place your pieces right sides together, and place them to the side of your sewing machine. Pin the pieces together, away from the area of the ¼" seam allowance. Lower the presser foot and stitch onto your leader. Begin feeding the pieces under the presser foot one after the other. If you choose to pin your pieces along the ¼" seam allowance, remove the pins before sewing. *Do not sew over pins.* Continue sewing your quilt pieces in this manner until you have sewn all of the pieces required for that specific part of your project. Sew onto another leader, and cut the threads between the pieces you have just sewn. Press seam allowances as indicated in the instructions.

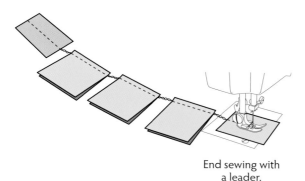

End sewing with
a leader.

I always chain stitch onto a small scrap of fabric, folded in half. It saves thread and allows me to continue piecing without raising and lowering the presser foot or stopping to trim threads. I never have to worry about the threads getting sucked into the bobbin casing or turning into a bird's nest on the back of my work. I also use a leader with the Quilt as You Go technique, and I even use a leader when I'm sewing garments and bags.

BACKSTITCHING NOT NEEDED

There's no need to backstitch, as you'll be stitching across each seam when piecing your quilt top. It may seem like I'm stating the obvious, but I had a student in one of my classes who was backstitching each of her seams as for garment sewing.

PRESS

You will hear quilters say this time and time again, "press your seams, iron your clothes." You'll never regret having invested in a heavy, hot iron. Use the heat and the weight of the iron to press your work. Ironing, or moving the iron back and forth over your work, could stretch and distort your fabrics. Get into the habit of pressing after sewing each seam. Crisply pressed seams will aid in your piecing accuracy. It's another one of those "best practices."

I usually press seam allowances in opposite directions from row to row. I like the way the opposing seams nestle together when the seam allowances are pressed in opposite directions. I seem to have better luck matching my points this way.

Opposing seams

Many people do, however, press their seam allowances open, and I do too, in some cases. Pressing seam allowances open when working with 30° triangles, 60° triangles, and hexagons will reduce the overall bulk in the seams. The debate on pressing seam allowances open or to one side is an ongoing one. Try both techniques and decide for yourself. In this book, you will find suggested pressing directions in the project instructions and illustrations.

1 Set your seam by pressing your pieces while they are still right sides together.

2 Referring to the pressing suggestions in the project instructions, flip open one side of the sewn piece with your fingers. Using the tip of the iron, press the seam allowances to one side, being careful to keep your fingers away from the iron. For a longer seam, press down on the seam, lift the iron, move it to the next part of the strip, and press down again, repeating until the entire piece is pressed.

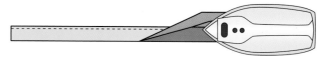

Don't slide iron. Press and lift.

APPLIQUÉ

There are many ways to appliqué, but the one I find to be most versatile is "needle-turn appliqué." You'll need only a straw needle, or milliner's needle, and some fine thread that matches the color of the appliqué.

After turning the edges under with the tip of the needle, stitch the appliqué with a blind stitch or a running stitch.

1. Trace the appliqué pattern onto the right side of your fabric. Cut out your appliqué shape approximately ⅛" to ¼" larger than the finished pattern.

2. Place the shape on the background fabric, and baste it in place.

3. Thread the appliqué needle with fine cotton or silk thread and knot the end. Bring the needle up from the wrong side of the background fabric and through the appliqué shape, just inside the turn-under line.

4. Use the tip of the needle to turn under the raw edge and use your non-sewing hand to hold the fold in place. Insert the needle down into the background fabric, and bring it back up about ¹⁄₁₆" away, through the folded edge of the appliqué. Continue to take small stitches in this manner.

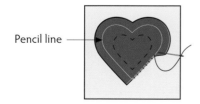

Pencil line

For reverse appliqué, layer the appliqué fabric under the background fabric, both with right sides facing up. Cut away the top fabric to reveal the appliqué fabric beneath.

Use the needle tip to turn under the seam allowance of the top fabric, and stitch using a blind stitch.

Quilt

The layers of a quilt include the top, the batting (inside layer), and a backing. They're basted together for hand or machine quilting, but kept separate if you intend to use the services of a long-arm machine quilter.

BACKING

Backing and batting requirements throughout this book are 4" to 6" larger than the completed quilt-top dimensions, leaving 2" to 3" on all sides. When piecing backing fabric, be sure to remove the selvages and sew the pieces together with a ½" seam allowance. Press the seam allowances open to reduce bulk. If you're having your quilt professionally machine quilted, check with your long-arm machine quilter to see what size the backing and batting should be. Adjust the backing yardage accordingly.

If you choose to hand quilt your project, hand baste the layers together with thread so that you can place your top in a hoop as you quilt.

If you want to machine quilt on your own sewing machine, pin baste the layers. If you use quilting safety pins that have a bend in them, you can easily remove them as you are quilting.

If you're preparing your top and backing for a long-arm quilter, press both of them carefully

TLC FOR QUILT TOPS

If you have completed a quilt top, but don't plan on quilting it right away, be sure it is folded so that the seams are protected. Fold the quilt top WRONG sides together, with the RIGHT side out. This will protect the seams from any wear and tear. Learn about storing quilt tops and quilts to best protect them from the elements that can damage your textiles. The International Quilt Study Center and Museum at University of Nebraska—Lincoln has a wealth of information on their website. Visit them at www.quiltstudy.org.

before sending the quilter your work. Your quilter will assemble the backing, batting, and top on the long-arm quilting machine. Be sure to discuss batting and thread options, as the quilter usually provides these for your project. Check the schedule of fees to see what options are available.

BASTING

Find a clean, dry place to work, preferably on a table so you don't have to work on the floor.

1 Press the backing with seam allowances open, to eliminate bulk. Place it right side down on your work surface. Using painter's tape, tape all sides to the surface. Place a longer piece of tape marking the center of the backing. Leave the corners free to avoid unnecessary stretching.

2 Place the batting on top of the backing, smoothing out any wrinkles. Tape the batting in the same manner as you did the backing. Again, use a longer piece of tape to mark the center.

3 Fold the finished quilt top in half horizontally, right sides together. Place the fold along the center of the taped backing and batting. Open the folded top, gently placing it right side up on the batting, and smoothing it out as you go. Do not tug or stretch it. Be sure it's placed squarely on your batting and backing.

4 Begin basting all three layers together with thread for hand quilting or with safety pins for machine quilting. Begin in the center of the quilt, and work out toward the edges, pinning or stitching every 5" to 7".

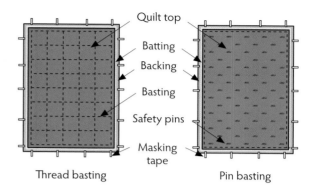

Thread basting   Pin basting

Quilt top
Batting
Backing
Basting
Safety pins
Masking tape

HAND QUILTING

I can tell you, jokingly, that quilting is nothing more than a running stitch, but that really wouldn't be completely true. I highly recommend taking a class in hand quilting at your local quilt shop. Or take one offered by your quilt guild or while attending a conference. Learn how to hand quilt, how to "rock" the needle, from a master of the craft. Have someone show you how to use a quilt hoop or frame and stitch north, south, east, and west. Sit quietly and just watch someone quilt. Absorb the rhythm and grace that slowing down and hand quilting can create.

There's a saying, "the smaller the needle, the smaller the stitch" but start out with a size 9 or 10 Between needle until you get the hang of it. The main thing is to try to keep your stitches even, and just enjoy the slower process. Here's what you'll need for hand quilting:

- Needles called Betweens
- Quilting hoop
- Hand-quilting thread such as Aurifil wool or Mako Egyptian cotton
- Thimble

For big-stitch hand quilting, the technique is the same, but you'll use a larger needle and heavier thread such as pearl cotton. I don't use a hoop for big-stitch quilting, but you may want to try it both ways to see which method you prefer. Here's what you'll need for big-stitch quilting:

- Crewel or embroidery needles, size 7
- Pearl cotton #8
- Thimble
- Quilting hoop (optional)

MACHINE QUILTING

If you want to stitch straight stitches through your quilt top, the best way to do that is with a walking foot. This foot will help move all three quilt layers along evenly. If you want to try free-motion quilting

on a sewing machine, you'll need a darning foot and a machine that has the option of lowering the feed dogs. Refer to your sewing-machine manual for more specific details.

Again, I would highly recommend taking a class before jumping into this style of quilting. Make up some 18"-square samples of fabric, batting, and backing. Practice before you start quilting an actual quilt top. Finally, just because you have decided to machine quilt a project, doesn't mean you have to rush through it. Slow down. Practice. Try different batting types. And again, take a class at a shop, a quilt guild, or a conference.

Here's what you'll need:

- Topstitch needles 80/12 or quilting needles 70/10
- Machine-quilting thread
- Walking foot

For free-motion quilting, you'll need:

- Darning foot
- Ability to lower feed dogs
- Gloves for gripping the quilt

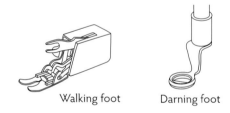

Walking foot   Darning foot

Feed dogs

LONG-ARM MACHINE QUILTING

Long-arm machine quilting has become an art in itself. The amount of time and effort that is devoted to machine quilting on a long-arm machine is just incredible. There are long-arm machine quilters who revel in the ability to add their touch to quilt tops, from simple to heirloom. They have an unwavering attention to detail and consistency, creating results that simply take your breath away.

If you're interested in trying a long-arm machine to quilt your own top, find a shop that not only rents time on a long-arm machine but also provides a good class in using it. To once again oversimplify, when you machine quilt on your home machine, you are moving the quilt. When you machine quilt on a long-arm machine, you are moving the machine. What a polar shift! Well worth a class, I'd say.

Finish

There is nothing more fulfilling than getting to this part of the process in your quiltmaking. So many people worry about how to bind a quilt. Think of it as a last chance to add a little color, contrast, or composition. And, remember to add a label.

BINDING

Use a walking foot when attaching the binding, and sew with a ¼" seam allowance. After the binding is sewn, turned to the back, and tacked down with a blind stitch, your quilt is complete! If you're giving your quilt as a gift, make a little extra binding and give it to the gift recipient for any future repairs that might be necessary. Remember, your quilt will probably last a lifetime.

1 Using a rotary cutter and ruler, trim the excess batting and backing even with the quilt top. For a fuller binding, I trim ¼" from the raw edge of the quilt top.

2 Cut straight-of-grain strips 2¼" x 42" as directed in each project. Trim the selvage from the strips. Sew the strips together at a 45° angle by placing them perpendicular to each other as shown. Sew from corner to corner, trim the excess fabric to leave a ¼" seam allowance, and press the seam allowances open to reduce bulk.

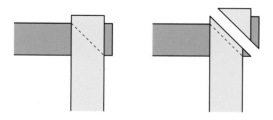

Joining straight-cut strips

3 Fold the strip in half lengthwise, wrong sides together, and press.

4 Place the raw edges of the binding on the front of your quilt, aligning them with the raw edge of your quilt top. Start stitching the binding to your quilt in the middle of one side of your quilt; leave a 12" length of the binding unsewn. Stitch until you're ¼" from the first corner.

5 With the needle up, lift the presser foot and turn the quilt so that the next edge of your quilt is to the right of your needle. Fold the binding up so that it aligns with the next raw edge as shown. Then fold the binding down onto itself and align the raw edges of the binding and quilt top. Make sure the fold that you have just made is even with the top of the quilt. Begin sewing the binding to the quilt again, using a ¼" seam allowance.

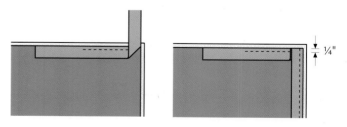

6 Continue sewing the binding, turning the corners in this manner until you are about 12" from your starting point. Overlap the two ends; trim both of the tails so that they overlap the same dimension as you used for the strip width of your binding. In this case, that would be 2¼".

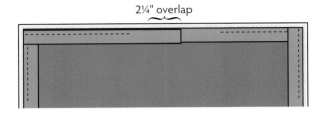

2¼" overlap

7 Unfold the strips and place them right sides together at a 90° angle. Stitch from corner to corner as you did when joining the strips. Trim the excess fabric and press the seam allowances open. Refold the strips and align the raw edges with the quilt top. Finish sewing this section to the quilt.

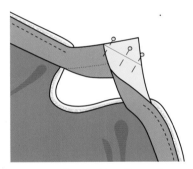

Draw diagonal line. Pin ends together, matching corners.

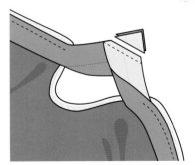

Stitch along line and trim excess.

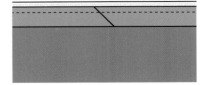

Refold binding and finish stitching to the quilt top.

8 Fold the pressed edge of the binding over the raw edges, to the back of the quilt, so that the pressed edge covers the machine stitching used to attach your binding. Stitch the edge to the back of your quilt using a small blind stitch.

 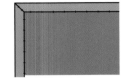

Quilt back

LABELS

Be sure to add a label to your quilt, either before or after quilting. Put your name, location, and date on the label with a little note to the intended recipient, if it is a gift. Even if your quilt is just for you, proudly put a label on your quilt, just for you!

PARTING NOTES

Believe in yourself.

Choose tools and techniques that you love.

Inspire someone by teaching them how to quilt; pass it on.

Make great quilts!!!

Resources

Most of the items listed below are available at independent quilt shops. By purchasing your products from these retailers, you'll be supporting a family of quilters, enabling them to continue to create wonderful quilts, offer great classes, and sponsor fabulous exhibits.

FABRICS

Alexander Henry Fabrics
www.ahfabrics.com

Robert Kaufman Fabrics
www.robertkaufman.com

Hoffman California Fabrics, International
www.hoffmanfabrics.com

Windham Fabrics
www.windhamfabrics.com

Dear Stella Design
www.dearstelladesign.com

THREAD

Aurifil
www.aurifil.com

Superior Threads
www.superiorthreads.com

TOOLS

Omnigrid cutting mats, rotary cutters, rulers
www.dritz.com

Creative Grids USA rulers
www.creativegridsusa.com

Jeana Kimball needles
www.jeanakimballquilter.com

Bohin needles and pins
www.bohin.fr/en/

Magid Roc gloves for machine quilting
www.magidglove.com

Quilters Dream batting
www.quiltersdreambatting.com

Easy Circle Cut Ruler
www.simplicity.com

Library

If you'd like to learn more about color, contrast, and composition, here's a short list of great titles for your library. Some titles may be out of print, but it's well worth searching for a used copy. Keep learning—take classes, join a guild, and enjoy the process of looking at things anew.

Albers, Josef and Nicholas Fox Weber. *Interaction of Color: 50th Anniversary Edition*. New Haven and London: Yale University Press, 2013.

Crow, Nancy. *NANCY CROW*. Elmhurst, Illinois: Breckling Press, 2006.

Crow, Nancy. *Improvisational Quilts: Renwick Gallery of the National Museum of American Art*. Concord, California: C & T Publishing, 1995.

Droste, Magdalena. *Bauhaus*. Koln: Taschen, 2006.

Ellis, Amy. *Think Big: Quilts, Runners, and Pillows from 18" Blocks*. Bothell, Washington: Martingale, 2014.

Hornung, David. *Color: A Workshop for Artists and Designers*. London: Lawrence King Publishing, 2013.

Hughes, Rose. *Design, Create, and Quilt: How to Design a Quilt—Lessons, Techniques, and Patterns*. Bothell, Washington: Martingale, 2012.

Hughes, Rose. *Exploring Embellishments: More Artful Quilts with Fast-Piece Appliqué*. Bothell, Washington: Martingale, 2010.

Huntley, H.E. *The Divine Proportion: A Study in Mathematical Beauty*. New York: Dover Publications, 1970.

Jinzenji, Yoshiko. *Quilting Line and Color: Techniques and Designs for Abstract Quilts*. Loveland, Colorado: Interweave, 2005.

Lupton, Ellen and J. Abbott Miller. *ABC's of the Bauhaus and Design Theory*. New York: Thames and Hudson, 1993.

Marks, Terry. *Color Harmony Compendium: A Complete Color Reference for Designers of All Types, 25th Anniversary Edition*. Beverly, Massachusetts: Rockport Publishers, 2009.

Marston, Gwen. *Liberated Quiltmaking*. Paducah, Kentucky: American Quilter's Society, 1996.

Schmidt, Denyse. *Denyse Schmidt Quilts: 30 Colorful Quilt and Patchwork Projects*. San Francisco, California: Chronicle Books, 2005.

Sherin, Aaris. *Design Elements: Color Fundamentals*. Beverly, Massachusetts: Rockport Publishers, 2012.

Walters, Angela. *Free-Motion Quilting with Angela Walters: Choose & Use Quilting Designs for Modern Quilts*. Concord, California: C & T Publishing, 2012.

Walters, Angela. *In the Studio with Angela Walters: Machine-Quilting Design Concepts Add Movement, Contrast, Depth, & More*. Concord, California: C & T Publishing, 2012.

About the Authors

Natalie Barnes

Natalie is the owner and designer for beyond the reef, a pattern-design company that she started one rainy north-shore morning while drinking coffee with author Jill Marie Landis on a lanai in Hanalei, Kauai. As a little girl, Natalie learned to sew, knit, and crochet from her grandmother. Later she began quilting with $.99 fabrics from Woolworth's. After a successful career in the demanding commercial-interior-design field in Los Angeles, Natalie decided it was time to step out in faith, live her dream, and put her talents to work in another area. She has never looked back. Having always lived on the beach, she draws her inspiration for color and design from the sea, the sky, and the land. These days you'll find Natalie in the studio in sunny Southern California, or out and about with Buddy-Dog.

Website: www.beyondthereefpatterns.com
Email: Natalie@beyondthereefpatterns.com
twitter: @beyondthereefca
facebook: facebook.com/beyondthereefpatterns
Instagram: instagram.com/beyondthereefpatterns

Angela Walters

Angela Walters is a long-arm quilter, teacher, and the author of two books. Her quilting career began at the side of her husband's grandfather, and together they made her first quilt, a nine-patch design that is still on her bed today. Thousands of swirls, feathers, and parallel lines later, she has turned her love of stitches and fabric into a thriving business focused on modern machine quilting. Angela also designs fabrics. She lives on the outskirts of Kansas City, Missouri, with her husband, three children, and many, many quilts.

Website: www.quiltingismytherapy.com